MW01610759

CHICAGO-AREA
GOLF COURSE GUIDE

Revised & Expanded Edition

Tim Tully

Chicago Review Press

Library of Congress Cataloging-in-Publication Data

Tully, Tim.
    Chicago-area golf course guide / Tim Tully. — Rev. and expanded
ed.
        p.   cm.
    Rev. ed. of: Chicago-area golf course guide / Terry Casey and Tim
Tully. c1990.
    Includes index.
    ISBN 1-55652-143-X : $9.95
    1. Golf courses—Illinois—Chicago Metropolitan Area—Directories.
I. Casey, Terry. Chicago-area golf course guide. II. Title.

GV983.C4C37   1992
796.352'068—dc20   92–198
                                                                    CIP

Published in 1992 by Chicago Review Press, Incorporated

814 North Franklin Street, Chicago, Illinois 60610

ISBN:1-55652-143-X

Contents

Introduction

According to the National Golf Foundation, there are about 1,370,000 golfers in the state of Illinois. Approximately ½—or 685,000—of these golfers live in the Chicago metropolitan area, and that number is expected to increase by 2 to 5 percent annually through the end of the century.

The Chicago area offers some of the finest public courses in the country to accommodate the growing number of golfers in the region. There are layouts to satisfy everyone's tastes and abilities, from long and challenging championship courses to short 9-hole, par-3 courses for the beginner or high handicapper.

This new, expanded edition of the *Chicago-Area Golf Course Guide* lists more than 150 public courses and includes information on rates, location, number of holes, personnel, and a brief course description. Every effort was made to obtain the most accurate and up-to-date information; however, the fees listed are subject to change. We strongly recommend that you call any course you plan to visit to schedule a tee time, especially on weekends.

I hope that this guide will provide an exciting variety of courses to the amateur and seasoned golfer alike.

Chicago Park District

COLUMBUS PARK GOLF COURSE
5700 WEST JACKSON BLVD.
CHICAGO, IL 60644
(312)294-2274

9-Hole Course, 2,867 Yards, Par 34, CDGA rating N/A
LOCATION: 8 miles west of the Loop
SEASON: April 1 through 1st week of November
COURSE OWNER: Chicago Park District
GREENS SUPERINTENDENT: Walter Clark

This 9-hole course is well suited to the high handicapper. The terrain is flat, and the fairways are wide open. Greens are small with few hazards. Only 9 sand traps and 1 water hazard come into play. The rough is kept fairly light to keep play moving.

SCORECARD:

HOLE	1	2	3	4	5	6	7	8	9	TOTAL
YARDS	330	157	433	310	443	340	267	200	387	2,867
PAR	4	3	4	4	4	4	4	3	4	34

RATES: Weekdays: residents, $6; nonresidents, $7; senior citizens, $4. Weekends: residents, $7; nonresidents, $8; senior citizens, $5.
FACILITIES: Snack shop, club rental; tee times must be purchased in advance through Ticketmaster at (312)559-1212.

JACKSON PARK GOLF COURSE
63RD STREET AND STONY ISLAND AVENUE
CHICAGO, IL 60637
(312)294-2274

18-Hole Course, 5,538 Yards, Par 69, CDGA rating N/A
LOCATION: 9 miles south of the Loop on South Lake Shore Drive
SEASON: April 1 through 1st week of November
COURSE OWNER: Chicago Park District
GREENS SUPERINTENDENT: John Brown

This 18-hole course is not long, and its fairways are flat and wide open. The medium-sized greens are well trapped, and new trees were planted in 1984 to make the course more challenging. Jackson Park is a good test for the average golfer.

SCORECARD:

HOLE	1	2	3	4	5	6	7	8	9	OUT
YARDS	400	364	289	290	425	183	363	140	312	2,766
PAR	4	4	4	4	4	3	4	3	4	34

HOLE	10	11	12	13	14	15	16	17	18	IN	TOTAL
YARDS	267	295	165	200	560	475	347	203	260	2,772	5,538
PAR	4	4	3	3	5	5	4	3	4	35	69

RATES: Weekdays: residents, $8; nonresidents, $9. Weekends: residents, $9; nonresidents, $10.
FACILITIES: Putting green, driving range, pro shop, snack shop, locker rooms, club rental; tee times must be purchased in advance through Ticketmaster at (312)559-1212.

MARQUETTE PARK GOLF COURSE
6700 SOUTH KEDZIE AVENUE
CHICAGO, IL 60629
(312)294-2274

9-Hole Course, 3,300 Yards, Par 36, CDGA rating N/A
LOCATION: Southwest Chicago
SEASON: April 1 through November
GOLF PROFESSIONAL: Tom Nicolini
COURSE OWNER: Chicago Park District
GREENS SUPERINTENDENT: Tom Fahey

This 9-hole Chicago Park District course features rolling hills and open fairways. Six sand traps and 350 new trees were added in 1989 making play more difficult, but the course is still well suited to the high handicapper. New tees and an irrigation system have also been added.

SCORECARD:

HOLE	1	2	3	4	5	6	7	8	9	TOTAL
YARDS	405	450	465	320	220	395	485	360	200	3,300
PAR	4	4	5	4	3	4	5	4	3	36

RATES: Weekdays: residents, $6; nonresidents, $7; senior citizens, $4. Weekends: residents, $7; nonresidents, $8; senior citizens, $5.

FACILITIES: Pro shop, restaurant, snack shop, club rental, golf equipment sold; tee times must be purchased in advance through Ticketmaster at (312)559-1212.

ROBERT A. BLACK GOLF COURSE
2045 WEST PRATT AVENUE
CHICAGO, IL 60645
(312)294-2294

9-Hole Course, 2,600 Yards, Par 33, CDGA rating N/A
LOCATION: 12 miles north of the Loop (6800 North)
SEASON: April 1 through November
COURSE OWNER: Chicago Park District
GREENS SUPERINTENDENT: Bob Lawson

Dick Nugent designed this 9-hole layout in 1974. Few trees line the watered fairways, and the large greens are well bunkered. There are no water holes to worry about on this hilly to gently rolling terrain, and excellent birdie opportunities are available on numbers 5, 6, and 9—all short par 4s. The high handicapper will enjoy this well-maintained park district course.

SCORECARD:

HOLE	1	2	3	4	5	6	7	8	9	TOTAL
YARDS	484	166	370	192	350	345	195	138	360	2,600
PAR	5	3	4	3	4	4	3	3	4	33

RATES: Weekdays: residents, $6; nonresidents, $7; senior citizens, $4. Weekends: residents, $7; nonresidents, $8; senior citizens, $5.
FACILITIES: Putting green, pro shop, snack shop, club rental, golf equipment sold; tee times must be purchased in advance through Ticketmaster at (312)559-1212.

SOUTH SHORE COUNTRY CLUB
7059 SOUTH LAKE SHORE DRIVE
CHICAGO, IL 60649
(312)294-2274

9-Hole Course, 2,903 Yards, Par 33, CDGA rating N/A
LOCATION: 12 miles south of the Loop
SEASON: April 1 through 1st week in November
COURSE OWNER: Chicago Park District
GREENS SUPERINTENDENT: Don Geraci

Now owned by the Chicago Park District, this 9-hole course was once a private country club. South Shore is not too long, and its watered fairways are heavily wooded and very narrow. The small greens are a tough target, and a good score requires straight, accurate shots. There are no water holes, but this tight course offers a stiff challenge for the medium to low handicapper.

SCORECARD:

HOLE	1	2	3	4	5	6	7	8	9	TOTAL
YARDS	360	445	445	378	173	426	193	335	148	2,903
PAR	4	4	4	4	3	4	3	4	3	33
HDCP	5	2	1	4	8	3	7	6	9	

RATES: Weekdays: residents, $6; nonresidents, $7; senior citizens, $4. Weekends: residents, $7; nonresidents, $8; senior citizens, $5.
FACILITIES: Banquet facilities; tee times must be purchased in advance through Ticketmaster at (312)559-1212.

SYDNEY A. MAROVITZ GOLF COURSE
3600 NORTH LAKE SHORE DRIVE
CHICAGO, IL 60613
(312)294-2274

9-Hole Course, 3,290 Yards, Par 36, CDGA rating N/A
LOCATION: 3 miles north of the Loop
SEASON: April 1 through November
GOLF PROFESSIONAL: Tom Nicolini
COURSE OWNER: Chicago Park District
GREENS SUPERINTENDENT: Bud Feid

This course was formerly called the Waveland Golf Course. When it was built, each hole was designed after one of the top holes in the United States. The terrain is flat, fairways are wide open, and all of the greens—which vary in size from small to large—are elevated and well bunkered. Over the years, 500 new trees have been planted, making this a true test of a good player's ability but still enjoyable for the average golfer.

SCORECARD:

HOLE	1	2	3	4	5	6	7	8	9	TOTAL
YARDS	410	485	175	435	525	135	420	320	385	3,290
PAR	4	5	3	4	5	3	4	4	4	36

RATES: Weekdays: residents, $6; nonresidents, $7; senior citizens, $4. Weekends: residents, $7; nonresidents, $8; senior citizens, $5.
FACILITIES: Golf lessons, pro shop, restaurant, snack shop, locker rooms, club rental, golf equipment sold, tee times must be purchased in advance through Ticketmaster at (312)559-1212.

Cook County
Forest Preserve

·:·

BILLY CALDWELL GOLF COURSE
6150 NORTH CALDWELL AVENUE
CHICAGO, IL 60646
(312)792-1930

9-Hole Course, 3,029 Yards, Par 35, CDGA rating N/A
LOCATION: 2 blocks west of the Edens expressway
SEASON: April or May until the 1st snow
COURSE OWNER: Cook County Forest Preserve
GREENS SUPERINTENDENT: Robert DeFigilia

This 9-hole Cook County Forest Preserve course is somewhat hilly, with open fairways and few hazards; water comes into play on only 1 hole. Greens are medium sized, and the rough is kept fairly light to keep play moving. Advance tee times are not available—play works on a first-come, first-served basis.

SCORECARD:

HOLE	1	2	3	4	5	6	7	8	9	TOTAL
YARDS	393	373	283	388	299	154	377	394	368	3,029
PAR	4	4	4	4	4	3	4	4	4	35
HDCP	2	6	4	3	8	9	5	1	7	

RATES: Weekdays: $6; senior citizens (with card), $3; juniors (under 17 with card), $3. Weekends: $8. Carts: hand carts, $1.75 per round. Senior citizen cards can be purchased for $3 for 3 years at Cook County Forest Preserve courses.
FACILITIES: Putting green, pro shop, snack shop, club rental, golf equipment sold.

BURNHAM WOODS GOLF COURSE
14201 BURNHAM AVENUE
BURNHAM, IL 60633
(708)862-9043

18-Hole Course, 6,480 Yards, Par 72, CDGA rating 68.0
LOCATION: 20 miles south of Chicago
SEASON: April through November
COURSE OWNER: Cook County Forest Preserve
GREENS SUPERINTENDENT: Edward Percak

Built in 1927 and designed by Stanley Pelcher, this has always been a public course. In 1948, the Cook County Forest Preserve District took over the course from the Village of Burnham. Since that time mature trees have been planted, making 7 fairways narrower. A lake was also added along the 9th fairway. The terrain is flat and there are no sand traps, although there are many grass bunkers around the small greens. Creeks wind through the course, coming into play on 11 holes. Burnham is well suited to the medium to high handicapper.

SCORECARD:

HOLE	1	2	3	4	5	6	7	8	9	OUT
YARDS	441	321	180	558	146	415	490	338	414	3,303
PAR	4	4	3	5	3	4	5	4	4	36
HDCP	5	13	16	1	18	6	3	12	7	

HOLE	10	11	12	13	14	15	16	17	18	IN	TOTAL
YARDS	392	369	147	478	363	296	225	380	527	3,177	6,480
PAR	4	4	3	5	4	4	3	4	5	36	72
HDCP	8	10	17	4	11	14	15	9	2		

RATES: Weekdays: $8; after 4 p.m., $7; senior citizens (with card), $4; juniors (under 17 with card), $4. Weekends: $10. Carts: $16; hand carts, $1.75. Senior citizen cards can be purchased for $3 for 3 years at Cook County Forest Preserve courses.

FACILITIES: Putting green, pro shop, snack shop, club rental, golf equipment sold.

"CHICK" EVANS GOLF COURSE
6145 GOLF ROAD
MORTON GROVE, IL 60053
(708)965-5353

18-Hole Course, 5,691 Yards, Par 71, CDGA rating N/A
LOCATION: 1 mile west of Old Orchard Shopping Mall
SEASON: April through November
COURSE OWNER: Cook County Forest Preserve
GREENS SUPERINTENDENT: Rick Krier

The north branch of the Chicago River winds through this 18-hole layout, coming into play on 5 holes. Mature trees line the fairways, but there are no sand traps to worry about. Six of the 18 holes offer doglegs leading to small greens. The terrain is flat, and the course is short and mostly wide open so scoring well should not be a problem here.

SCORECARD:

HOLE	1	2	3	4	5	6	7	8	9	OUT
YARDS	339	324	487	149	377	340	327	294	378	3,015
PAR	4	4	5	3	4	4	4	4	4	36
HDCP	7	10	1	18	4	6	9	13	3	

HOLE	10	11	12	13	14	15	16	17	18	IN	TOTAL
YARDS	155	351	331	313	486	278	307	287	168	2,676	5,691
PAR	3	4	4	4	5	4	4	4	3	35	71
HDCP	17	5	8	11	2	15	12	14	16		

RATES: Weekdays: $8; after 4 p.m., $7; senior citizens (with card), $4; juniors (under 17 with card), $4. Weekends: $10. Carts: $16; hand carts, $2. Senior citizen cards can be purchased for $3 for 3 years at Cook County Forest Preserve courses.

FACILITIES: Putting green, pro shop, snack shop, club rental, golf equipment sold.

EDGEBROOK GOLF COURSE
5900 North Central Avenue
Chicago, IL 60646
(312)763-8320

18-Hole Course, 4,626 Yards, Par 66, CDGA rating N/A
LOCATION: 10 miles northwest of the Loop
SEASON: April through November
COURSE OWNER: Cook County Forest Preserve District
GREENS SUPERINTENDENT: Phil Parker

This 18-hole executive course has 12 par-4 and 6 par-3 holes. The Chicago River cuts through the course, creating hazards on 3 holes. Trees line several fairways, which vary from tight to open, and the rough is kept fairly light. Greens are medium sized and well kept, and there are no sand traps to catch your approach shots. This course is well suited to the high handicapper.

SCORECARD:

HOLE	1	2	3	4	5	6	7	8	9	OUT
YARDS	268	234	321	264	93	230	151	287	297	2,145
PAR	4	3	4	4	3	3	3	4	4	32
HDCP	10	13	4	11	18	14	17	6	5	

HOLE	10	11	12	13	14	15	16	17	18	IN	TOTAL
YARDS	174	255	269	368	153	387	277	276	322	2,481	4,626
PAR	3	4	4	4	3	4	4	4	4	34	66
HDCP	15	12	9	2	16	1	7	8	3		

RATES: Weekdays: $8; after 4 p.m., $7; senior citizens (with card), $4; juniors (under 17 with card), $4. Weekends: $10. Carts: $16; hand carts, $2. Senior citizen cards can be purchased for $3 for 3 years at Cook County Forest Preserve courses.

FACILITIES: Pro shop, restaurant, snack shop, club rental, golf equipment sold.

THE GEORGE W. DUNNE
NATIONAL GOLF COURSE
16310 SOUTH CENTRAL AVENUE
OAK FOREST, IL 60452
(708)429-6886

18-Hole Course, 7,170 Yards, Par 72, CDGA rating 75.1
LOCATION: 15 miles south of the Loop
SEASON: April through November
GOLF PROFESSIONAL: George Kallish
COURSE OWNER: Cook County Forest Preserve
GREENS SUPERINTENDENT: Ralph Morrone

Dick Nugent and Ken Killian designed this beautiful championship course, which opened in 1982. Built on almost 300 acres, it was formerly called the Forest Preserve National Golf Course. It may now be the finest municipal course in the world. With 4 sets of tees on each hole, this course offers a true test for the serious golfer. Eight lakes, 64 sand bunkers, and large rolling greens add to the challenge. A 42-tee lighted driving range and 2 large putting greens make this a complete golfing facility. The George W. Dunne National is definitely not for the duffer. Greens superintendent, Ralph Morrone, advises that you "bring a lot of balls" if you plan on playing here. Tee times are required and must be scheduled on the day that you play.

SCORECARD:

HOLE	1	2	3	4	5	6	7	8	9	OUT
GOLD	545	410	165	430	415	570	190	390	440	3,555
BLUE	520	385	145	400	385	545	170	360	430	3,340
WHITE	490	360	125	370	355	515	140	330	410	3,095
RED	445	315	115	345	325	485	105	300	355	2,790
PAR	5	4	3	4	4	5	3	4	4	36
HDCP	7	13	17	3	9	1	15	11	5	

HOLE	10	11	12	13	14	15	16	17	18	IN	TOTAL
GOLD	440	540	400	185	550	450	395	205	450	3,615	7,170
BLUE	415	510	365	155	525	420	365	175	420	3,350	6,690
WHITE	390	460	345	135	495	390	330	145	390	3,080	6,175
RED	320	405	315	115	465	355	295	120	355	2,745	5,535
PAR	4	5	4	3	5	4	4	3	4	36	72
HDCP	10	2	12	18	6	8	14	16	4		

RATES: Weekdays: $12; after 4 p.m., $10; senior citizens (with card), $6; juniors (under 17 with card), $6. Weekends: $16. Carts: $16; hand carts, $2. Senior citizen cards can be purchased for $3 for 3 years at Cook County Forest Preserve courses. There is a $4 surcharge for nonresidents of Cook County.

FACILITIES: Putting green, driving range, golf lessons, pro shop, snack shop, club rental, golf equipment sold, tee time required.

HIGHLAND WOODS GOLF COURSE
2775 NORTH ELA ROAD
HOFFMAN ESTATES, IL 60195
(708)359-5850

18-Hole Course, 6,510 Yards, Par 72, CDGA rating 71.6
LOCATION: 35 miles northwest of the Loop
SEASON: March through November
COURSE OWNER: Cook County Forest Preserve
GREENS SUPERINTENDENT: Craig Meissner

This course was designed by William J. Spear and opened in 1976. Since its construction, several trees have been added, which will make the course considerably tougher once they mature. The watered fairways are wide, and the terrain is slightly hilly. The greens are mostly large and well trapped. Large fairway traps can also cause some problems. The lagoons situated on the course create hazards on 6 holes, and several doglegs test your accuracy. This forest preserve golf course is kept in very good condition and is well suited to the average golfer.

SCORECARD:

HOLE	1	2	3	4	5	6	7	8	9	OUT
CHAMP	420	530	380	170	440	550	370	200	410	3,470
REG.	395	500	345	150	420	520	330	180	380	3,220
WOMEN	360	460	320	120	390	500	290	140	350	2,930
PAR	4	5	4	3	4	5	4	3	4	36
HDCP	8	6	12	18	4	2	14	16	10	

HOLE	10	11	12	13	14	15	16	17	18	IN	TOTAL
CHAMP	415	530	390	225	465	550	360	185	405	3,525	6,995
REG.	395	500	355	190	440	530	340	160	380	3,290	6,510
WOMEN	375	445	315	155	390	510	310	125	340	2,965	5,895
PAR	4	5	4	3	4	5	4	3	4	36	72
HDCP	7	5	11	13	3	1	15	17	9		

RATES: Weekdays: $12; after 4:00 p.m., $10; senior citizens (with card), $6; juniors (under 17 with card), $6. Weekends: $16. Carts: $16; hand carts, $2. Senior citizen cards can be purchased for $3 for 3 years at Cook County Forest Preserve courses.
FACILITIES: 2 putting greens, driving range, golf lessons, pro shop, snack shop, club rental, golf equipment sold.

INDIAN BOUNDARY GOLF COURSE
8600 WEST FOREST PRESERVE DRIVE
CHICAGO, IL 60634
(312)625-1233

18-Hole Course, 5,991 Yards, Par 70, CDGA rating 69.5

LOCATION: Northwest side of Chicago next to River Grove, Schiller Park (O'Hare)

SEASON: Mid-March until the 1st snow

COURSE OWNER: Cook County Forest Preserve

GREENS SUPERINTENDENT: Marcelo Vargas

Indian Boundary was built in the 1920s and acquired by the Forest Preserve during the Depression. New greens, sand traps, tees, and hilly terrain were added in 1988 with plans for the entire course to be redone under USGA specifications in the next few years. Golf course architect Dick Nugent has designed the changes. The fairways are wide and separated by openly spaced, new trees with a few more mature stands. Except for the 4 new holes—numbers 5 through 8—the course is flat with grassy bunkers and roll-up greens. It is easy to walk and is very popular with senior citizens. All tees, except 5 through 8, are paved with either rubber or Astroturf driving-range-type mats.

SCORECARD:

HOLE	1	2	3	4	5	6	7	8	9	OUT
YARDS	414	301	462	322	189	305	337	136	418	2,884
PAR	4	4	5	4	3	4	4	3	4	35
HDCP	4	18	2	10	12	14	8	16	6	

HOLE	10	11	12	13	14	15	16	17	18	IN	TOTAL
YARDS	352	361	388	323	465	170	422	206	420	3,107	5,991
PAR	4	4	4	4	5	3	4	3	4	35	70
HDCP	13	9	7	15	1	17	3	11	5		

RATES: Weekdays: $8; after 4 p.m., $7; senior citizens (with card), $4; juniors (under 17 with card), $4. Weekends: $10. Carts: $16; hand carts, $2. Senior citizen cards can be purchased for $3 for 3 years at Cook County Forest Preserve courses.

FACILITIES: Putting green, pro shop, snack shop, club rental, golf equipment sold.

JOE LOUIS GOLF COURSE
13100 SOUTH HALSTED STREET
RIVERDALE, IL 60627
(708)849-1731

18-Hole Course, 6,391 Yards, Par 72, CDGA rating N/A
LOCATION: 20 miles south of the Loop
SEASON: April through November
GOLF PROFESSIONAL: Harry Collins
COURSE OWNER: Cook County Forest Preserve
GREENS SUPERINTENDENT: Fred Marberry

The terrain on this course is flat, and 3 lakes come into play on several holes. The large greens are well trapped, and the fairways are tree lined but wide open. From the championship tees, these 18 holes are long and challenging. Every hole is modeled after one from a major golf course in the United States, and all tees are named after famous black athletes. Watch out for Jackie Robinson and Lee Elder! Tee times are available on a first-come, first-served basis.

SCORECARD:

HOLE	1	2	3	4	5	6	7	8	9	OUT
CHAMP	383	367	430	150	560	438	614	169	351	3,462
REG.	365	332	395	143	518	420	587	158	329	3,247
WOMEN	297	275	316	120	424	338	474	128	266	2,638
PAR	4	4	4	3	5	4	5	3	4	36
HDCP	10	17	6	14	8	4	1	16	18	

HOLE	10	11	12	13	14	15	16	17	18	IN	TOTAL
CHAMP	344	383	386	186	529	552	432	159	436	3,407	6,869
REG.	309	352	367	157	505	523	406	124	401	3,144	6,391
WOMEN	251	311	302	130	432	420	327	105	332	2,610	5,248
PAR	4	4	4	3	5	5	4	3	4	36	72
HDCP	15	11	13	7	2	5	9	12	3		

RATES: Weekdays: $12; after 4 p.m., $10; senior citizens (with card), $6; juniors (under 17 with card), $6. Weekends: $16. Carts: $16; hand carts, $2. Senior citizen cards can be purchased for $3 for 3 years at Cook County Forest Preserve courses.
FACILITIES: Putting green, golf lessons, pro shop, restaurant, snack shop, club rental, golf equipment sold.

MEADOW LARK GOLF COURSE
11599 WEST 31ST STREET
HINSDALE, IL 60521
(708)562-2977

9-Hole Course, 3,333 Yards, Par 36, CDGA rating N/A
LOCATION: 16 miles west of the Loop
SEASON: Late March through early December
COURSE OWNER: Cook County Forest Preserve
GREENS SUPERINTENDENT: Ira Fagel

This 9-hole Forest Preserve course was built in 1965 and has always been a public property. The terrain is basically flat, and the fairways are wide open from fenceline to fenceline. There are no sand traps or grass bunkers to worry about and only 1 large pond which creates a hazard on 2 holes. This is one of the busiest 9-hole courses in the area: more than 72,000 rounds were played in 1988.

SCORECARD:

HOLE	1	2	3	4	5	6	7	8	9	TOTAL
YARDS	428	415	470	170	395	555	351	203	346	3,333
PAR	4	4	5	3	4	5	4	3	4	36
HDCP	6	3	1	5	2	9	7	8	4	

RATES: Weekdays: $6; senior citizens (with card), $3; juniors (under 17 with card) 10 a.m.–3 p.m., $3. Weekends: $8. Carts: $8; hand carts, $1.50. Senior citizen cards can be purchased for $3 for 3 years at Cook County Forest Preserve courses.

FACILITIES: Putting green, pro shop, snack shop, club rental, golf equipment sold.

RIVER OAKS GOLF COURSE
1 PARK AVENUE
CALUMET CITY, IL 60409
(708)868-4090

18-Hole Course, 6,416 Yards, Par 72, CDGA rating 70.0
LOCATION: 10 miles south of the Loop, 4 miles from Indiana
SEASON: April through December
GOLF PROFESSIONAL: Cliff Brown
COURSE OWNER: Cook County Forest Preserve
GREENS SUPERINTENDENT: James E. Bennett, Sr.

In 1982 the Urban Development Corporation donated this 18-hole course to the Cook County Forest Preserve District. Built in 1971 and designed by Ken Killian and Dick Nugent, River Oaks is situated near the Little Calumet River on 8½ acres of gently rolling terrain. The fairways are narrow and dotted with sand traps. Greens are medium to large and well trapped, making it difficult to pitch and roll onto them. You don't have to be a heavy hitter to score well here, but the course demands accuracy to avoid the many water hazards and large oak trees. The large ponds come into play on 15 out of the 18 holes. This course is well suited to the low handicapper, and the greens fees are very low—especially for the caliber of this course.

SCORECARD:

HOLE	1	2	3	4	5	6	7	8	9	OUT
GOLD	353	350	212	525	415	198	324	484	407	3,268
RED	330	327	148	474	380	157	308	466	377	2,967
PAR	4	4	3	5	4	3	4	5	4	36
HDCP	9	10	15	2	4	17	14	8	7	

HOLE	10	11	12	13	14	15	16	17	18	IN	TOTAL
GOLD	165	501	335	339	355	549	354	172	415	3,185	6,453
RED	139	461	318	322	328	510	337	140	375	2,930	5,897
PAR	3	5	4	4	4	5	4	3	4	36	72
HDCP	16	5	13	12	6	1	11	18	3		

RATES: Weekdays: $8; after 4 p.m., $7; senior citizens (with card), $4; juniors (under 17 with card), $4. Weekends: $10. Carts: $16; hand carts, $1.75. Senior citizen cards can be purchased for $3 for 3 years at Cook County Forest Preserve courses.
FACILITIES: Putting green, pro shop, snack shop, club rental, golf equipment sold.

South

BALMORAL WOODS COUNTRY CLUB
2500 BALMORAL WOODS DRIVE
CRETE, IL 60417
(708)672-7448

18-Hole Course, 6,477 Yards, Par 72, CDGA rating 72.5
LOCATION: 45 minutes south of Chicago on IL 394
SEASON: April through November
GOLF DIRECTOR: David Mortell
COURSE OWNER: Don Mortell
GREENS SUPERINTENDENT: Bob Morrell

Balmoral Woods is a challenging course with a good variety of holes ranging from short par 3s to long par 5s. The terrain is hilly, and the holes are beautifully laid out. Fairways are a combination of narrow and open, and the greens vary from small to large. There are 9 water hazards and 30 sand traps on this demanding but fair 6,477-yard course. Balmoral Woods hosted the 1985 Chicago Open, and Stan Utley shot the course record with a 64.

SCORECARD:

HOLE	1	2	3	4	5	6	7	8	9	OUT
BLUE	543	337	515	429	193	430	526	155	497	3,625
WHITE	531	322	490	416	182	420	518	138	481	3,498
RED	400	260	460	355	130	340	400	113	380	2,838
PAR	5	4	5	4	3	4	5	3	5	38
HDCP	5	15	9	7	13	3	1	17	11	

HOLE	10	11	12	13	14	15	16	17	18	IN	TOTAL
BLUE	443	186	510	212	300	469	171	324	443	3,058	6,683
WHITE	432	179	500	204	290	459	164	319	432	2,979	6,477
RED	335	135	420	140	276	347	119	312	330	2,414	5,252
PAR	4	3	5	3	4	4	3	4	4	34	72
HDCP	6	12	10	8	16	2	14	18	4		

RATES: Weekdays: $23 for 18; $29 with cart; $15 walking; $22 with cart after 3 p.m. Seniors $14 walking; $20 with cart. Weekends: $30 with cart (required before 2 p.m.); $28 walking; $29 with cart after 2 p.m.
FACILITIES: Putting green, driving range, golf lessons, pro shop, restaurant, snack shop, bar, banquet facilities, locker rooms, club rental, golf equipment sold, cart required on weekends, tee time recommended, permanent tee time available.

BON VIVANT GOLF CLUB
Career Center Road
Bourbonnais, IL 60914
(815)935-0403 or (800)248-7775

18-Hole Course, 7,014 Yards, Par 72, CDGA rating 73.7
LOCATION: 48 miles south of the Loop
SEASON: April 1 through November 30
GOLF PROFESSIONAL: John Krutilla
COURSE OWNER: Merlin Karlock
GREENS SUPERINTENDENT: Jim Miller

Totaling just over 7,000 yards from the men's tees and nearly 7,500 yards from the championship tees, Bon Vivant is one of the longest courses in the Chicago area. Built in 1979 and maturing nicely, the course is situated on slightly rolling terrain and features wide-open fairways that tend to narrow as they approach the large greens. There are 57 strategically placed sand traps and bunkers that dot the fairways and protect the greens. Nine water hazards can create problems and dominate the back 9, where 6 holes are affected. Bon Vivant is a test of both accuracy and strength.

SCORECARD:

HOLE	1	2	3	4	5	6	7	8	9	OUT
CHAMP	360	570	446	241	595	479	200	445	462	3,798
MEN	339	542	411	213	571	454	176	415	439	3,560
WOMEN	315	456	308	162	470	434	157	319	420	3,041
PAR	4	5	4	3	5	4	3	4	4	36
HDCP	15	5	11	13	1	3	17	7	9	

HOLE	10	11	12	13	14	15	16	17	18	IN	TOTAL
CHAMP	598	419	403	200	348	442	233	469	588	3,700	7,498
MEN	566	395	378	171	325	411	201	447	560	3,454	7,014
WOMEN	467	314	358	158	304	299	138	429	471	2,938	5,979
PAR	5	4	4	3	4	4	3	4	5	36	72
HDCP	2	8	12	18	16	10	14	4	6		

RATES: Weekdays: $12 for 18, $7 for 9. Weekends: $18 for 18, $10 for 9. Carts: weekdays, $14 for 18, $8 for 9; weekends, $16 for 18, $9 for 9.
FACILITIES: Putting green, driving range, golf lessons, pro shop, restaurant, snack shop, bar, banquet facilities, locker rooms, club rental, golf equipment sold, tee time recommended.

CHERRY HILLS COUNTRY CLUB
191ST STREET AND KEDZIE AVENUE
FLOSSMOOR, IL 60422
(708)799-5600

18-Hole Course, 6,270 Yards, Par 72, CDGA rating 69.6
9-Hole Executive Course, 2,267 Yards, Par 33, CDGA rating N/A
LOCATION: 25 miles south of the Loop
SEASON: Open all year
COURSE OWNER: Corporate owned
GREEN SUPERINTENDENT: Dale Pieper

Built in 1926, the original 18-hole layout at Cherry Hills was designed by Harry Collins and Jack Daray, Sr., with an adjoining 9-hole course added in 1966. The area is wooded, displaying a variety of trees, and the terrain is relatively flat with some rolling hills. The fairways are broad, and the elevated undulating greens range from medium to large in size. Water is not much of a factor on the course, but the 50 well-positioned sand traps and grass bunkers will affect your score. The course has excellent drainage allowing for year-round and wet-weather play. Cherry Hills is in great condition, affording an enjoyable round for all golfers.

SCORECARD:

HOLE	1	2	3	4	5	6	7	8	9	OUT
WHITE	447	403	353	185	341	288	205	389	454	3,065
RED	428	394	327	161	331	277	186	383	437	2,924
PAR	5	4	4	3	4	4	3	4	5	36
HDCP	7	3	9	15	13	17	5	1	11	

HOLE	10	11	12	13	14	15	16	17	18	IN	TOTAL
WHITE	489	381	349	375	300	133	562	199	417	3,205	6,270
RED	435	355	328	360	283	113	518	157	399	2,948	5,872
PAR	5	4	4	4	4	3	5	3	4	36	72
HDCP	12	4	14	10	16	18	8	6	2		

EXECUTIVE COURSE SCORECARD:

HOLE	1	2	3	4	5	6	7	8	9	TOTAL
YARDS	274	128	295	133	342	145	167	471	312	2,267
PAR	4	3	4	3	4	3	3	5	4	33
HDCP	5	9	3	6	2	8	7	1	4	

RATES: Weekdays: $18 for 18; after 3 p.m., $12.50; after 6 p.m., $8.50. Weekends: $21 for 18; after 3 p.m., $12.50; after 6 p.m., $8.50. Seniors: $11. 9-hole executive course: weekdays, $9; weekends, $10.50. Carts: weekdays, $20 for 18, $9.50 for 9; weekends, $21.

FACILITIES: 2 putting greens, pro shop, restaurant, bar, banquet facilities, locker rooms, club rental, golf equipment sold, tee time recommended, permanent tee time available.

DEER CREEK GOLF CLUB
26201 SOUTH WESTERN AVENUE
UNIVERSITY PARK, IL 60466
(708)672-6667

18-Hole Course, 6,755 Yards, Par 72, CDGA rating 72.3
LOCATION: 33 miles south of the Loop
SEASON: Open all year
GOLF PROFESSIONAL: Jim Formas
COURSE OWNER: Jerry Kaufman
GREENS SUPERINTENDENT: Mark Nebesnyk

Deer Creek is long, totaling just under 6,800 yards from the championship tees. The course is laid out on a combination of rolling hills and flat terrain that provides excellent drainage and allows for wet-weather play. The watered fairways are wide open, leading up to large greens, and the course has few trees but an abundance of sand. A total of 53 traps are placed strategically in the fairways and around the greens. Seven water hazards add to the difficulties on the course, making Deer Creek one of the most competitive in the area.

SCORECARD:

HOLE	1	2	3	4	5	6	7	8	9	OUT
BLUE	423	370	496	145	377	556	443	208	402	3,420
WHITE	403	350	476	122	351	535	423	186	379	3,225
RED	369	307	440	99	325	500	381	154	356	2,931
PAR	4	4	5	3	4	5	4	3	4	36
HDCP	5	15	7	17	13	3	1	9	11	

HOLE	10	11	12	13	14	15	16	17	18	IN	TOTAL
BLUE	373	514	414	163	418	349	536	182	386	3,335	6,755
WHITE	354	492	393	144	410	325	512	167	396	3,193	6,518
RED	321	453	355	125	382	301	488	142	337	2,904	5,835
PAR	4	5	4	3	4	5	5	3	36	72	
HDCP	16	10	4	18	2	14	12	8	6		

RATES: Weekdays: $13 for 18, $7.75 after 3 p.m. and for 9. Weekends: $18.25 for 18, $13 after 2 p.m., $8.50 after 4 p.m., $10 for 9. Carts: weekdays: $18 for 18, $9.50 for 9; weekends: $19 for 18, $9.50 for 9.
FACILITIES: Putting green, driving range, golf lessons, pro shop, restaurant, snack shop, bar, banquet facilities, locker rooms, club rental, golf equipment sold, fivesomes allowed, tee time recommended, permanent tee time available.

GLENWOODIE CLUB
193RD AND STATE STREETS
GLENWOOD, IL 60425
(708)758-1212

18-Hole Course, 6,423 Yards, Par 72, CDGA rating 71.8
LOCATION: 24 miles south of the Loop
SEASON: Open all year
GOLF PROFESSIONAL: Dave Mose
COURSE OWNER: Joe Jemsek
GREENS SUPERINTENDENT: Rory Bancroft

Glenwoodie was built in the mid-1930s and is run by Joe Jemsek under a lease arrangement. The course is completely watered and superbly conditioned with fairways so lush that the ball rolls very little after landing. This causes the course to play longer than the 6,670 yards listed on the scorecard. The fairways on the front 9 are mostly flat, while the back 9 features slightly more hilly terrain. Water comes into play on 7 holes, and the large, elevated greens can be tough to read. Overall, Glenwoodie is challenging for the better golfer but playable for the majority.

SCORECARD:

HOLE	1	2	3	4	5	6	7	8	9	OUT
CHAMP	411	386	184	533	157	339	535	348	380	3,273
REG.	407	370	149	521	146	325	524	332	365	3,139
WOMEN	355	302	158	469	119	284	463	285	313	2,748
PAR	4	4	3	5	3	4	5	4	4	36
HDCP	6	10	16	4	18	12	2	14	8	

HOLE	10	11	12	13	14	15	16	17	18	IN	TOTAL
CHAMP	454	386	133	499	206	415	430	332	542	3,397	6,670
REG.	441	372	121	486	195	395	418	321	535	3,284	6,423
WOMEN	387	328	94	449	165	304	335	238	457	2,757	5,505
PAR	4	4	3	5	3	4	4	4	5	36	72
HDCP	7	9	17	5	15	13	1	11	3		

RATES: Weekdays: $17 for 18, $12 after 2 p.m., $10 after 4 p.m., $7.50 after 6 p.m. Weekends: $20.50 for 18, $14.50 after 2 p.m., $11.50 after 4 p.m., $7.50 after 6 p.m. Carts: $20 for two riders, $14 for single riders.
FACILITIES: Putting green, driving range, golf lessons, pro shop, snack shop, bar, locker rooms, club rental, golf equipment sold, fivesomes allowed with carts, tee time recommended, permanent tee time available on weekends.

GREEN GARDEN COUNTRY CLUB
MANHATTAN-MONEE AND CENTER ROAD
FRANKFORT, IL 60423
(815)469-3350

18-Hole Course, 6,563 Yards, Par 72, CDGA rating 68.9
LOCATION: 22 miles south of the Loop
SEASON: April through November
GOLF PROFESSIONAL: Ralph Krueger
COURSE OWNERS: Dennis Piotrowski and Bill McEnery
GREENS SUPERINTENDENT: Herb Gerlock

Green Garden Country Club was built in 1973 on a combination of rolling hills and flat terrain. The bluegrass fairways range from narrow to medium in size, and the bent-grass greens are large and elevated. Water is the primary concern on the course with 3 lakes and 1 creek affecting 8 holes, 5 of which are on the back 9. The course ends with a difficult dogleg right par 4 that requires an accurate drive and a strong approach shot to reach the green. The condition of the course has improved considerably over the past 2 years. New tees, a new clubhouse, and a new driving range have been added, and more extensive course renovations are planned for the near future.

SCORECARD:

HOLE	1	2	3	4	5	6	7	8	9	OUT
BLUE	519	351	178	494	471	446	184	331	435	3,409
WHITE	505	344	166	478	459	433	168	319	420	3,292
RED	491	326	76	407	373	360	137	309	365	2,844
PAR	5	4	3	5	4	4	3	4	4	36
HDCP	7	15	13	9	1	3	11	17	5	

HOLE	10	11	12	13	14	15	16	17	18	IN	TOTAL
BLUE	502	354	153	419	335	314	324	331	422	3,154	6,563
WHITE	488	342	137	407	321	304	312	320	408	3,039	6,331
RED	455	330	121	397	310	236	300	310	394	2,853	5,697
PAR	5	4	3	4	4	4	4	4	4	36	72
HDCP	6	10	18	4	8	16	14	12	2		

RATES: Weekdays: $18 for 18; $12 after 3 p.m.; $9 for 9; seniors, $9 for 18 holes. Weekends: $22 for 18; $12 after 3 p.m.; $11 for 9. Carts: weekdays, $18 for 18, $9 for 9; weekends, $22.
FACILITIES: Putting green, driving range, golf lessons, pro shop, restaurant, snack shop, bar, banquet facilities, locker rooms, club rental, golf equipment sold, tee time recommended, permanent tee time available.

HICKORY HILLS COUNTRY CLUB
8201 WEST 95TH STREET
HICKORY HILLS, IL 60457
(708)598-6460

18-Hole Course, 6,018 Yards, Par 71, CDGA rating 67.9
9-Hole Course, 1,630 Yards, Par 29, CDGA rating N/A
LOCATION: 15 miles southwest of the Loop, 1 mile west of I-294
SEASON: Open all year
GOLF PROFESSIONAL: George Gianakas
COURSE OWNER: Steven P. Gianakas
GREENS SUPERINTENDENT: Peter Gianakas

Designed by James Foulis, Jr., and built in 1925, Hickory Hills has matured into a championship-quality golf course. A 9-hole, par-29 course was later added to accommodate more golfers. The holes are beautifully laid out on very hilly terrain; an abundance of mature oak, maple, elm, and willow trees dominates the landscape. The fairways are open, but accurate tee shots are required to score well here. The greens are small, though not well bunkered, and water comes into play on just a few holes. The course has a variety of short and long par 4s testing both accuracy and strength. Hickory Hills offers large banquet facilities and is planning a new 40,000-square-foot clubhouse that will overlook the entire course.

SCORECARD:

HOLE	1	2	3	4	5	6	7	8	9	OUT
YARDS	512	355	320	145	422	451	172	368	304	3,049
PAR	5	4	4	3	4	5	3	4	4	36
HDCP	2	9	13	17	6	4	15	8	11	

HOLE	10	11	12	13	14	15	16	17	18	IN	TOTAL
YARDS	134	428	528	168	458	424	312	150	367	2,969	6,018
PAR	3	4	5	3	5	4	4	3	4	35	71
HDCP	18	5	1	16	3	7	10	14	12		

HOLE	1	2	3	4	5	6	7	8	9	TOTAL
YARDS	150	178	135	116	195	175	169	294	218	1,630
PAR	3	3	3	3	3	3	3	4	4	29
HDCP	6	4	8	9	2	5	7	1	3	

RATES: Weekdays: $20 for 18, $13 for 9, $12 after 2 p.m. Weekends: $24 for 18, $15 after 3 p.m. 9-hole course: $8 at all times. Carts: weekdays, $20; weekends, $24 for 18, $14 for 9.

FACILITIES: 2-tiered, lighted driving range with 72 pads, putting green, pro shop, restaurant, snack shop, bar, banquet facilities, locker rooms, club rental, golf equipment sold, cart required, tee time required, permanent tee time available.

LINCOLN OAKS GOLF COURSE
390 EAST RICHTON ROAD
CRETE, IL 60417
(708)672-9401

18-Hole Course, 6,298 Yards, Par 72, CDGA rating 69.3

LOCATION: 2½ miles east of Route 394

SEASON: March 1 through November

GOLF PROFESSIONAL: Jay Williams

The challenging Lincoln Oaks course was built in 1927. The terrain consists of rolling hills, and the watered fairways are a combination of tight and open. The greens are small and fairly well protected by most of the 56 sand traps placed on the course. The area is wooded but water only affects holes 5, 7, and 13. The back 9 plays longer than the front, featuring 4 par 5s. Play finishes with the longest par 5 on the course, requiring an accurate drive and 2 good shots to reach the green. Lincoln Oaks provides a good test for the average golfer.

SCORECARD:

HOLE	1	2	3	4	5	6	7	8	9	OUT
BLUE	368	190	411	169	496	163	478	338	372	2,985
WHITE	363	187	409	167	491	155	475	335	362	2,944
RED	358	116	406	163	477	147	463	332	352	2,814
PAR	4	3	4	3	5	3	5	4	4	35
HDCP	8	10	2	16	4	18	6	14	12	

HOLE	10	11	12	13	14	15	16	17	18	IN	TOTAL
BLUE	335	344	491	166	511	185	529	201	551	3,313	6,298
WHITE	328	341	487	161	500	173	516	183	548	3,237	6,181
RED	320	338	483	91	489	161	503	164	498	3,047	5,861
PAR	4	4	5	3	5	3	5	3	5	37	72
HDCP	15	13	7	17	5	11	1	9	3		

RATES: Weekdays: $14 for 18; $8.50 after 3 p.m.; $7.50 for 9; seniors, $9.50. Weekends: $18.50 for 18, $10.50 after 3 p.m. Carts: $10 per person for 18, $6.50 per person for 9.

FACILITIES: Putting green, driving range, golf lessons, pro shop, restaurant, bar, banquet facilities, golf equipment sold, tee time required, permanent tee time available.

LONGWOOD COUNTRY CLUB
3200 EAST STEGER ROAD
STEGER, IL 60475
(708)758-1811

18-Hole Course, 6,025 Yards, Par 70, CDGA rating 69.0

LOCATION: 3 miles east of Route 394 on Steger Road
SEASON: Open all year
GOLF PROFESSIONAL: Joe Tintari
COURSE OWNER: Tintari family
GREENS SUPERINTENDENT: George Hernandez

Located on hilly terrain, Longwood offers a challenging variety of holes that tests both accuracy and strength. The fairways range from tight to open, and the trees are few but large. The medium-sized greens are elevated and protected by 40 to 50 bunkers placed on the course. A number of holes requires high approach shots to avoid the traps that are situated in front of the greens. Nine tees are being enlarged, and a new watering system was recently installed to include the fairways.

SCORECARD:

HOLE	1	2	3	4	5	6	7	8	9	OUT
BLUE	430	330	205	540	445	350	445	160	350	3,255
WHITE	410	320	195	470	435	335	430	150	340	3,085
RED	385	308	185	400	380	290	415	140	290	2,793
PAR	4	4	3	5	4	4	4	3	4	35
HDCP	7	17	11	1	3	13	5	15	9	

HOLE	10	11	12	13	14	15	16	17	18	IN	TOTAL
BLUE	365	180	405	505	465	420	345	325	160	3,170	6,425
WHITE	330	155	390	490	455	355	340	280	145	2,940	6,025
RED	310	140	380	485	445	350	330	275	140	2,855	5,648
PAR	4	3	4	5	4	4	4	4	3	35	70
HDCP	8	12	6	2	4	10	14	18	16		

RATES: Weekdays: $14; $11 after 2 p.m.; seniors, $9. Weekends: $18, $15 after noon, $13 after 2 p.m. Carts: $20.

FACILITIES: Putting green, driving range, golf lessons, pro shop, restaurant, bar, banquet facilities, locker rooms, club rental, fivesomes allowed, tee time recommended, permanent tee time available.

McARTHUR MUNICIPAL GOLF COURSE
140TH STREET AND INDIANAPOLIS BLVD.
EAST CHICAGO, IN 46312
(219)391-8362

9-Hole Course, 1,404 Yards, Par 30, CDGA rating N/A
LOCATION: 15 miles southeast of the Loop
SEASON: April 1 until Labor Day
PARKS SUPERINTENDENT: Richard Gomez

McArthur Municipal is a short, 9-hole course situated on mostly flat terrain with some rolling hills and an average amount of trees. The watered fairways are narrow, and the small greens are bunkerless with the exception of 3 holes. This is basically an iron course, and many players use it to work on their short game.

SCORECARD:

HOLE	1	2	3	4	5	6	7	8	9	TOTAL
REG.	120	215	146	247	158	192	120	111	95	1,404
PAR	3	4	3	4	3	4	3	3	3	30

RATES: Weekdays: residents, $1 for 18; nonresidents, $3. Weekends: residents, $1.25 for 18; nonresidents, $3.
FACILITIES: Putting green, golf lessons, snack shop, club rental.

MINNIE MONESSE GOLF CLUB
R.R. #1, P.O. Box 465
Grant Park, IL 60940
(815)465-6653

18-Hole Course, 6,120 Yards, Par 71, CDGA rating 68.1

LOCATION: 45 miles southeast of downtown Chicago

SEASON: April through October

GOLF PROFESSIONAL: Mark English

COURSE OWNER: Edward J. Hurley

GREENS SUPERINTENDENT: Jim Gerlack

Minnie Monesse Golf Club is one of the most scenic and challenging golf courses in the Chicago area. The terrain is hilly, and the watered fairways are relatively narrow. The course is heavily wooded with a variety of mature trees covering the layout. The bent grass greens are moderately bunkered, with water coming into play on 11 holes. The course's par-3 4th hole and the par-5 8th are 2 of the most difficult holes on Chicago-area public golf courses. Minnie Monesse actually dates back to before World War II when it was a tough 9-hole course. It changed hands during the war and became a turkey farm, reopening as a golf course in 1961.

SCORECARD:

HOLE	1	2	3	4	5	6	7	8	9	OUT
MEN	405	325	310	210	510	200	310	500	135	2,905
WOMEN	395	325	310	200	450	200	310	500	110	2,800
PAR	4	4	4	3	5	3	4	5	3	35
HDCP	3	11	15	5	7	9	13	1	17	

HOLE	10	11	12	13	14	15	16	17	18	IN	TOTAL
MEN	425	357	425	469	400	182	300	337	320	3,215	6,120
WOMEN	400	357	410	469	400	166	290	337	301	3,130	5,930
PAR	4	4	4	5	4	3	4	4	4	36	71
HDCP	4	8	2	10	6	18	14	12	16		

RATES: Weekdays: $14 for 18, $10 for 9, $9 after 3 p.m. Seniors: $30 for 2 players with cart. Weekends: $18 for 18, $12 for 9 and after 3 p.m. Carts: $16 for 18, $8 for 9.

FACILITIES: Putting green, golf lessons, pro shop, snack shop, bar, banquet facilities, locker rooms, club rental, golf equipment sold, fivesomes allowed, tee time recommended, permanent tee time available.

OAK SPRINGS GOLF COURSE
R.R. #1, BOX 343
ST. ANNE, IL 60964
(815)937-1648

18-Hole Course, 6,354 Yards, Par 72, CDGA rating 69.6
LOCATION: 10 miles southeast of Kankakee
SEASON: April 1 through November 15
GOLF MANAGER: Ed Kuncel
DIRECTOR OF GOLF: Rick Dauphin
COURSE OWNER: Spring Creek Recreation, Inc.
GREENS SUPERINTENDENT: Bart Schaaf

Oak Springs is long, totaling just under 6,800 yards from the championship tees. The front 9 was heavily wooded when the course was built in 1969, and the trees planted on the back side at the time of construction have matured and come into play. The terrain is hilly with relatively narrow watered fairways. There are 31 sand traps and 5 water hazards strategically placed throughout the course. One of the most difficult holes is the 425-yard, par-4 5th hole. The fairway is tree lined and extremely narrow, requiring precision. Oak Springs is challenging and well worth the drive south.

SCORECARD:

HOLE	1	2	3	4	5	6	7	8	9	OUT
BLUE	520	180	520	450	460	362	373	230	450	3,545
WHITE	510	170	510	430	425	347	363	200	391	3,346
RED	500	160	500	333	399	332	353	170	377	3,124
PAR	5	3	5	4	4	4	4	3	4	36
HDCP	9	13	7	3	1	5	17	11	15	

HOLE	10	11	12	13	14	15	16	17	18	IN	TOTAL
BLUE	316	420	558	345	135	387	140	518	420	3,239	6,784
WHITE	306	387	514	330	125	369	132	478	367	3,008	6,354
RED	300	370	422	314	113	352	124	471	345	2,811	5,935
PAR	4	4	5	4	3	4	3	5	4	36	72
HDCP	14	2	4	12	18	6	8	10	16		

RATES: Weekdays: $10 for 18; $5.50 after 4 p.m.; seniors, $8 for 18. Tuesday/Friday special, $26 for 2 players with cart. Weekends: $14 for 18, $7 after 4 p.m. Carts: $12 for 18, $6 for 9; seniors, $10 for 18, $5 for 9.
FACILITIES: Putting green, driving range, golf lessons, pro shop, restaurant, snack shop, bar, banquet facilities, locker rooms, tee time required on weekends, tee time recommended.

PALMIRA GOLF COURSE
12111 WEST 109TH STREET
ST. JOHN, IN 46373
(219)365-4331

18-Hole Course, 6,444 Yards, Par 71, CDGA rating 70.9
LOCATION: 45 minutes southeast of the Loop
SEASON: April through December
GOLF PROFESSIONAL: Rich Nicpon
COURSE OWNER: A. P. Bonaventura
GREENS SUPERINTENDENT: Rich Nicpon

Built in 1972, Palmira—a long, somewhat difficult course—is situated on 140 acres of land. Mild hills make up the terrain, and the bluegrass fairways are wide open. The course has a good amount of trees, and the bent-grass greens are medium to large in size. The greens were recently reconstructed and are in excellent condition. The course has just 12 sand traps, and water affects only a few holes. Play finishes with a 151-yard par 3 that offers a good birdie opportunity.

SCORECARD:

HOLE	1	2	3	4	5	6	7	8	9	OUT
YARDS	383	170	551	426	409	125	360	369	339	3,132
PAR	4	3	5	4	4	3	4	4	4	35
HDCP	17	14	3	15	4	7	16	8	5	

HOLE	10	11	12	13	14	15	16	17	18	IN	TOTAL
YARDS	310	367	165	493	440	416	390	580	151	3,312	6,444
PAR	4	4	3	5	4	4	4	5	3	36	71
HDCP	11	1	2	9	10	18	12	6	13		

RATES: Weekdays: $11 for 18; $8 for 9; seniors, $7 for 18. Saturdays: $15 for 18, $10 for 9; after 2 p.m.: $12 for 18, $8 for 9. Sundays: $16 for 18; $12 after 2 p.m.; $10 for 9. Senior citizens: $2 off regular weekend prices. Carts: weekdays, $17; weekends, $18.

FACILITIES: Putting green, driving range, pro shop, snack shop, bar, club rental, golf equipment sold, tee time required on weekends, tee time recommended, permanent tee time available.

SCHERWOOD GOLF COURSE
600 East Joliet Street
Schererville, IL 46375
(219)865-2554

18-Hole Course, 6,256 Yards, Par 72, CDGA rating 69.5
9-Hole Course, 1,291 Yards, Par 27, CDGA rating N/A
LOCATION: 30 miles southeast of the Loop, 1 mile east of U.S. 41
SEASON: Open all year
GOLF PROFESSIONAL: Mark Beggs
COURSE OWNER: Marv Hanson
GREENS SUPERINTENDENT: Ron Hanson

Scherwood is a well-groomed, quality golf course situated on 170 acres of flat terrain. The 18-hole course was built in 1967, and the 9-hole par 3 was added in 1974. The course comprises wide driving areas and large, elevated, flat greens. The bluegrass fairways are tree lined, providing fairway definition, and there are 11 water hazards and 54 sand traps mainly around the greens. Scherwood is a popular facility for large outings and features a banquet hall, picnic area, and outdoor swimming pool.

SCORECARD:

HOLE	1	2	3	4	5	6	7	8	9	OUT
GOLD	346	403	476	175	385	153	488	398	415	3,239
BLUE	336	378	472	145	360	138	480	376	369	3,054
RED	312	284	430	104	271	117	436	268	308	2,530
PAR	4	4	5	3	4	3	5	4	4	36
HDCP	14	4	12	16	2	18	10	6	8	

HOLE	10	11	12	13	14	15	16	17	18	IN	TOTAL
GOLD	502	413	503	196	373	187	470	456	371	3,471	6,710
BLUE	471	380	471	175	353	169	425	422	336	3,202	6,256
RED	359	314	435	130	270	105	344	352	261	2,570	5,100
PAR	5	4	5	3	4	3	4	4	4	36	72
HDCP	11	5	13	7	15	9	1	3	17		

PAR-3 SCORECARD:

HOLE	1	2	3	4	5	6	7	8	9	TOTAL
REG.	156	149	132	188	142	97	152	149	126	1,291
PAR	3	3	3	3	3	3	3	3	3	27
HDCP	3	6	4	1	7	9	2	5	8	

RATES: Weekdays: $13 for 18, $8 for 9, $7.50 after 4 p.m. Seniors: $10 for 18, $7 for 9. Weekends: $18 for 18, $13 after 1 p.m. 9-hole par 3: $4.50; replay, $2.75. Carts: $18 for 18, $9 for 9.

FACILITIES: Putting green, driving range, golf lessons, pro shop, restaurant, snack shop, bar, banquet facilities, locker rooms, golf equipment sold, tee time recommended, permanent tee time available.

SHADY LAWN GOLF COURSE
615 DIXIE HIGHWAY
BEECHER, IL 60401
(708)946-2800

North: 9-Hole Course, 3,118 Yards, Par 36, CDGA rating N/A
Center: 9-Hole Course, 3,118 Yards, Par 36, CDGA rating N/A
South: 9-Hole Course, 3,177 Yards, Par 36, CDGA rating N/A
LOCATION: 30 minutes south of Chicago
SEASON: Open all year
GOLF PROFESSIONAL: Tony Holguin
COURSE OWNER: J. T. Wilkes
GREENS SUPERINTENDENT: Jerry Crist

Shady Lawn features 27 holes of gently rolling terrain with broad fairways and a combination of small and large greens. There are many mature trees on the layout but very little water to worry about. The greens are moderately bunkered with 35 well-placed sand traps on the course. The original 18 holes were designed by R. A. Anderson in the mid-1920s, and the 3rd 9 was added in 1986. Shady Lawn offers an enjoyable round of golf and earned its nickname as "the friendly course" because of the courteous service golfers receive.

NORTH COURSE SCORECARD:

HOLE	1	2	3	4	5	6	7	8	9	TOTAL
BLUE	375	175	379	516	420	135	530	279	309	3,118
RED	351	164	329	484	361	110	480	269	277	2,825
PAR	4	3	4	5	4	3	5	4	4	36
HDCP	5	8	2	3	1	9	4	7	6	

CENTER COURSE SCORECARD:

HOLE	1	2	3	4	5	6	7	8	9	TOTAL
BLUE	375	168	360	523	433	471	133	475	180	3,118
RED	309	155	330	493	403	451	132	445	160	2,878
PAR	4	3	4	5	4	5	3	5	3	36
HDCP	4	8	5	2	1	3	9	6	7	

SOUTH COURSE SCORECARD:

HOLE	1	2	3	4	5	6	7	8	9	TOTAL
BLUE	412	329	332	430	131	500	160	333	550	3,177
RED	382	299	302	400	127	465	140	313	470	2,898
PAR	4	4	4	4	3	5	3	4	5	36
HDCP	4	6	5	3	9	1	8	7	2	

RATES: Before March 29: Weekdays: $8 for 18. Monday and Friday: $30 for 2 golfers, cart included. Weekends: $11 for 18, $8 for 9, $9 after 1 p.m., $8 after 3 p.m. Carts: weekdays, $15; weekends, $17.

March 29 through April 27: Weekdays: $12 for 18, $9 after 1 p.m. Monday and Friday: $32 for 2 golfers, cart included. Weekends: $15 for 18, $9 for 9, $12 for 18 after 1 p.m., $9 after 3 p.m. Carts: weekdays, $16; weekends, $18.

April 27 through September 29: Weekdays: $13.50 for 18; $8 before 7:30 a.m.; $10.50 after 1 p.m.; $7.50 after 3 p.m.; senior citizens, $9; juniors, $7.50 after 1 p.m. 9-hole rate: $7.50. Weekends: $18.50 for 18; $15.50 after 1 p.m.; $9.75 after 3 p.m.; senior citizens, $14 noon to 3 p.m. 9-hole rate: $11. Carts: weekdays, $18; $16.50 before 7:30 a.m.; weekends, $19.50.

September 30 through October 21: Weekdays: $10 for 18, $6 for 9, $8 after 1 p.m. Monday and Friday: $29 for 2 golfers, cart included. Weekends: $15 for 18, $9 for 9, $12 after 1 p.m., $9 after 3 p.m. Carts: weekdays, $16; weekends, $18.

FACILITIES: Putting green, golf lessons, pro shop, restaurant, snack shop, bar, banquet facilities, locker rooms, club rental, golf equipment sold, fivesomes allowed, tee time recommended, permanent tee time available.

SHAMROCK GOLF CLUB
ROUTE 6, BOX 255
ST. ANNE, IL 60964
(815)937-9355

18-Hole Course, 3,657 Yards, Par 60, CDGA rating N/A
LOCATION: 5 miles east of Kankakee on Route 17
SEASON: Open all year
GOLF PROFESSIONAL: Larry Horrell
COURSE OWNER: Mary LeBeau

Shamrock is a short, scenic course totaling just over 3,650 yards built along the Kankakee River. It is heavily wooded with tight tree-lined fairways set on flat terrain. The greens are flat, medium in size, and basically open with very few bunkers. With a par of 60 and holes ranging from 110 to 337 yards, the course is great for beginners and for working on your short game.

SCORECARD:

HOLE	1	2	3	4	5	6	7	8	9	OUT
YARDS	317	150	180	337	173	250	150	150	290	1,997
PAR	4	3	3	4	3	4	3	3	4	31
HDCP	4	9	3	1	7	17	14	13	16	

HOLE	10	11	12	13	14	15	16	17	18	IN	TOTAL
YARDS	300	153	158	173	160	133	133	110	340	1,660	3,657
PAR	4	3	3	3	3	3	3	3	4	29	60
HDCP	5	10	11	6	8	15	9	18	2		

RATES: Weekdays: $8 for 18; $5 after 4 p.m.; $6 for 9. Weekends: $9 for 18. Carts: $10 for 18; $6 for 9; pull carts, $1.
FACILITIES: Putting green, snack shop, locker rooms, club rental.

SILVER LAKES COUNTRY CLUB
147TH STREET AND 82ND AVENUE
ORLAND PARK, IL 60462
(708)349-6944

North: 18-Hole Course, 6,485 Yards, Par 72, CDGA rating 70.4
South: 18-Hole Course, 5,948 Yards, Par 70, CDGA rating 67.9
Rolling Hills: 9-Hole Course, 1,587 Yards, Par 29, CDGA rating 27.1
LOCATION: 45 minutes southwest of the Loop
SEASON: Open all year
GOLF PROFESSIONAL: Gregg Tingerstrom
GREENS SUPERINTENDENT: Dudley Smith

Silver Lakes offers 45 holes of golf for everyone from the beginner to the long hitter. The 9-hole Rolling Hills Course is a short par-3 layout, while the North Course is long with wide-open fairways and 3 water hazards. Although the greens are well protected by sand traps, accuracy is not as important as distance on the North layout. Golfers with the ability to hit accurate tee shots and high, soft approach shots will want to play the South Course, which is considerably shorter and tighter than the North Course. Water comes into play on 7 holes, and the rolling terrain means you'll have plenty of uphill and downhill lies. The large greens are elevated and difficult to read because of the number of breaks you'll encounter. Silver Lakes is a very well maintained, beautifully scenic course that has been a favorite of golfers in the Chicago area since it opened as a private club in 1921.

NORTH SCORECARD:

HOLE	1	2	3	4	5	6	7	8	9	OUT
BLUE	403	447	528	132	318	404	493	385	470	3,580
WHITE	382	427	493	122	304	382	483	331	458	3,382
RED	361	407	436	112	290	319	473	319	399	3,116
PAR	4	4	5	3	4	4	5	4	4	37
HDCP	9	1	5	17	15	7	11	13	3	

HOLE	10	11	12	13	14	15	16	17	18	IN	TOTAL
BLUE	441	421	168	348	433	469	439	379	148	3,246	6,826
WHITE	428	401	148	343	406	459	417	358	143	3,103	6,485
RED	389	381	108	285	379	449	395	283	107	2,776	5,892
PAR	4	4	3	4	4	5	4	4	3	35	72
HDCP	2	4	18	14	8	10	2	12	16		

SOUTH SCORECARD:

HOLE	1	2	3	4	5	6	7	8	9	OUT
WHITE	562	331	129	339	522	370	164	390	226	3,033
RED	503	319	114	311	500	352	143	372	204	2,818
PAR	5	4	3	4	5	4	3	4	3	35
HDCP	1	13	17	11	5	7	15	3	9	

HOLE	10	11	12	13	14	15	16	17	18	IN	TOTAL
WHITE	405	300	459	172	358	168	531	379	143	2,915	5,948
RED	282	188	445	120	278	130	509	365	118	2,435	5,253
PAR	4	4	5	3	4	3	5	4	3	35	70
HDCP	2	10	6	16	12	14	4	8	18		

ROLLING HILLS SCORECARD:

HOLE	1	2	3	4	5	6	7	8	9	TOTAL
WHITE	119	171	237	302	149	158	173	123	155	1,587
PAR	3	3	4	4	3	3	3	3	3	29
HDCP	17	11	3	1	13	7	9	15	5	

RATES: Weekdays: $20.50 for 18, $11 after 3 p.m., $8 on Rolling Hills 9. Weekends: $24 for 18, $14 after 3 p.m., $9 on Rolling Hills 9. Carts: $21 for 18, $13 for 9.

FACILITIES: Putting green, driving nets, golf lessons, pro shop, restaurant, snack shop, bar, banquet facilities, locker rooms, club rental, golf equipment sold, tee time recommended.

SOUTH GLEASON GOLF COURSE
3400 SOUTH JEFFERSON STREET
GARY, IN 46408
(219)980-1089

18-Hole Course, 6,312 Yards, Par 71, CDGA rating 69.0
LOCATION: 33 miles southeast of the Loop
SEASON: April 1 through October 31
GOLF PROFESSIONAL: John Lowe
COURSE OWNER: City of Gary
GREENS SUPERINTENDENT: Riley Vickrey

Built in 1928, South Gleason has matured nicely. The terrain is flat, and the fairways are a mixture of broad and narrow. Straight tee shots are required in order to avoid the thick roughs which flank the fairways. The course has few trees and only 3 sand traps, but quite a few grass bunkers. The greens are small and are tough targets for approach shots. The front 9 is long, totaling 3,422 yards from the back tees, while the back 9 is considerably shorter at just under 3,000 yards. Offering a variety of holes, South Gleason is enjoyable for players of all levels.

SCORECARD:

HOLE	1	2	3	4	5	6	7	8	9	OUT
WHITE	350	358	430	451	441	179	544	233	436	3,422
RED	340	348	420	441	431	169	534	223	426	3,332
PAR	4	4	4	5	4	3	5	3	4	36
HDCP	15	13	5	17	3	11	9	7	1	

HOLE	10	11	12	13	14	15	16	17	18	IN	TOTAL
WHITE	385	196	455	415	274	350	370	112	333	2,890	6,312
RED	375	186	445	405	264	340	360	102	323	2,800	6,132
PAR	4	3	5	4	4	4	4	3	4	35	71
HDCP	6	8	16	2	14	10	4	18	12		

RATES: Weekdays: $10 for 18, $6 for 9, $5 after 4 p.m., $5 for seniors and students. Weekends: $12 for 18, $6 after 3 p.m.
FACILITIES: Putting green, golf lessons, pro shop, restaurant, snack shop, club rental, golf equipment sold, tee time recommended, permanent tee time available.

SOUTH SHORE GOLF CLUB
ROUTE 2, BOX 176
MOMENCE, IL 60954
(815)472-4407

18-Hole Course, 6,226 Yards, Par 72, CDGA rating 68.1
LOCATION: North shore of Kankakee River, 3 miles west of Momence
SEASON: Open all year
COURSE OWNER: James H. Kasler
GREENS SUPERINTENDENT: James Bales

South Shore was built in 1927 and purchased in 1975 by the current owner. Each year since then has seen the addition of grass bunkers and 25 to 50 new trees. There is usually a brisk breeze blowing over the course, which is situated on land that is flat for the most part and not very heavily wooded. There are only 15 sand traps dotting the fairways and protecting the greens. Water is the main hazard you'll encounter here, with a creek that winds through the course affecting play on 7 holes and 4 small lakes creating trouble on 4 others. The course is not very long, and if you can avoid the water you should be able to score well here.

SCORECARD:

HOLE	1	2	3	4	5	6	7	8	9	OUT
WHITE	364	351	143	329	512	488	112	361	375	3,035
RED	338	330	137	276	439	455	105	345	325	2,750
PAR	4	4	3	4	5	5	3	4	4	36
HDCP	3	11	13	7	5	9	17	15	1	

HOLE	10	11	12	13	14	15	16	17	18	IN	TOTAL
WHITE	521	357	508	359	148	413	383	144	358	3,191	6,226
RED	439	308	460	316	118	348	278	137	311	2,715	5,465
PAR	5	4	5	4	3	4	4	3	4	36	72
HDCP	6	10	14	4	18	2	8	12	16		

RATES: Weekdays: $7 Monday and Friday; $10 Tuesday, Wednesday, and Thursday; $7 after 3 p.m. Weekends: $13, $8 after 2 p.m. Carts: $15, $12 Monday and Friday.
FACILITIES: Putting green, driving range, pro shop, restaurant, snack shop, bar, banquet facilities, club rental, golf equipment sold, tee time recommended, permanent tee time available.

TUCKAWAY GOLF COURSE
GOODENOW ROAD AND STONY ISLAND
CRETE, IL 60417
(708)946-2259

18-Hole Course, 6,185 Yards, Par 71, CDGA rating 68.7
LOCATION: 35 miles south of downtown Chicago
SEASON: Open all year
GOLF PROFESSIONAL: Marc Adduci
COURSE OWNER: Tuckaway, Inc.

Tuckaway is a beautifully maintained course located in a remote country setting. The tree-lined fairways roll gently up to small greens. Water comes into play on 3 holes, and the course toughens on the back 9 with the 10th, 11th, and 12th holes being long par 4s that demand accurate drives. Tuckaway is an enjoyable course for golfers of all levels.

SCORECARD:

HOLE	1	2	3	4	5	6	7	8	9	OUT
MEN	359	468	362	392	343	165	350	185	331	2,955
WOMEN	312	441	347	367	308	146	323	172	313	2,729
PAR	4	5	4	4	4	3	4	3	4	35
HDCP	7	11	5	1	13	15	3	9	17	

HOLE	10	11	12	13	14	15	16	17	18	IN	TOTAL
MEN	375	425	438	190	456	163	333	484	366	3,230	6,185
WOMEN	271	403	422	167	435	145	317	462	348	2,970	5,699
PAR	4	4	4	3	5	3	4	5	4	36	71
HDCP	4	6	2	12	14	18	16	8	10		

RATES: Weekdays: $12.50 for 18, $8.50 after 3 p.m., $8 for 9. Weekends: $17 for 18; $12.50 after 3 p.m. and for 9. Carts: weekdays: $19 for 18, $12 for 9; weekends: $20 for 18, $12 for 9.
FACILITIES: Putting green, driving range, golf lessons, pro shop, restaurant, bar, banquet facilities, locker rooms, club rental, golf equipment sold, tee time recommended, permanent tee time available.

URBAN HILLS COUNTRY CLUB
23520 CRAWFORD AVENUE
RICHTON PARK, IL 60471
(708)747-0306 OR (708)747-0603

18-Hole Course, 6,266 Yards, Par 71, CDGA rating 69.1
LOCATION: 30 miles south of the Loop
SEASON: Open all year
GOLF PROFESSIONAL: Bruce Meyer
COURSE OWNER: Wilma Urban
GREENS SUPERINTENDENT: Chuck Fogle

When construction began on the course in 1965, there was only 1 tree on what had previously been farmland. In the late 1970s, the tees were enlarged and extended, and many sand traps were added. Today, 20-year-old trees are becoming a factor on this relatively flat, open course. With 3 sets of tees to choose from, well-placed sand traps, and several small lakes and streams, there are enough challenging features at Urban Hills to test the mid- to low handicapper. The club also offers complete clubhouse facilities, and the restaurant features homemade soups, pies, and a wide assortment of moderately priced salads and sandwiches.

SCORECARD:

HOLE	1	2	3	4	5	6	7	8	9	OUT
BLUE	319	530	428	157	360	445	189	566	385	3,379
WHITE	303	507	407	138	324	424	176	468	367	3,114
GOLD	287	416	256	119	310	291	140	411	297	2,527
PAR	4	5	4	3	4	4	3	4	4	35
HDCP	15	11	5	17	13	1	9	3	7	

HOLE	10	11	12	13	14	15	16	17	18	IN	TOTAL
BLUE	322	197	328	464	426	351	626	158	399	3,271	6,650
WHITE	307	187	313	491	411	339	606	134	364	3,152	6,266
GOLD	292	177	298	391	346	327	532	110	266	2,739	5,266
PAR	4	3	4	5	4	4	5	3	4	36	71
HDCP	10	8	12	18	2	14	4	16	6		

RATES: Weekdays: $12 for 18, $9 after 2 p.m., $7 after 4 p.m., $7.50 for 9, $7 after 2 p.m. Weekends: $16 for 18, $12 after 2 p.m., $8 after 4 p.m., $10 for 9, $8 after 2 p.m. Carts: $18 for 18, $10 for 9.
FACILITIES: Putting green, golf lessons, pro shop, restaurant, snack shop, bar, banquet facilities, locker rooms, club rental, tee time required weekends, tee time recommended weekdays.

West & Southwest

ADDISON GOLF CLUB
19 WEST 250 ARMY TRAIL ROAD
ADDISON, IL 60101
(708)628-9713

9-Hole Course, 1,709 Yards, Par 27, CDGA rating N/A
LOCATION: 19 miles west of Chicago
SEASON: April through end of October
COURSE OWNER: Helen Byrne
GREENS SUPERINTENDENT: Thomas Byrne

Built in 1955 and designed by Mel Johnson, Addison is a par-3, 9-hole course with gently rolling terrain. Fairways are wide open, with a creek and pond coming into play on 4 holes. This executive course is not easy to par with 4 holes over 200 yards.

SCORECARD:

HOLE	1	2	3	4	5	6	7	8	9	OUT
WHITE	230	156	242	250	156	217	149	162	147	1,709
RED	208	119	242	250	156	217	149	112	147	1,600
PAR	3	3	3	3	3	3	3	3	3	27

RATES: Weekdays: $6.75, $6.25 replay. Weekends: $7.50, $7 replay.
FACILITIES: Putting green, pro shop, snack shop, bar, club rental, golf equipment sold.

ARROWHEAD GOLF CLUB
26 WEST 151 BUTTERFIELD ROAD
WHEATON, IL 60187
(708)653-5800

South: 9-Hole Course, 3,240 Yards, Par 35,CDGA rating 68.4
East: 9-Hole Course, 3,066 Yards, Par 35, CDGA rating 68.4
West: 9-Hole Course, 3,007 Yards, Par 35, CDGA rating 68.4
LOCATION: 30 miles west of the Loop
SEASON: Open all year
GOLF PROFESSIONAL: Pete Drogos
COURSE OWNER: Wheaton Park District
GREENS SUPERINTENDENT: Bob Breen

This course was originally the Elks Country Club and later became semiprivate Arrowhead before turning public. The Wheaton Park District purchased the course in 1982 from the Jansen family, who had owned it since the 1960s. Arrowhead has three 9-hole courses: South, East, and West.

The South and East courses have very small, slightly elevated greens and wide-open fairways, while the West has large rolling greens and tighter fairways. Sixty bunkers guard the 27 holes, and all fairways are bent grass. Water is not much of a factor here; there are only 5 small lakes over the 27 holes. The West course stays open all year on temporary greens, while the rest of the course is closed for cross-country skiing. Tee times are needed on weekends and strongly recommended at all times, as this is a very busy facility with more than 75,000 rounds played each year.

SOUTH SCORECARD:

HOLE	1	2	3	4	5	6	7	8	9	TOTAL
REG.	308	561	343	187	373	148	462	426	432	3,240
SHORT	294	548	336	129	303	140	449	420	426	3,045
PAR	4	5	4	3	4	3	4	4	4	35
HDCP	8	1	7	5	6	9	2	3	4	

EAST SCORECARD:

HOLE	1	2	3	4	5	6	7	8	9	TOTAL
REG.	481	364	173	416	396	313	130	377	416	3,066
SHORT	469	353	161	408	388	301	123	364	399	2,966
PAR	5	4	3	4	4	4	3	4	4	35
HDCP	3	6	4	1	5	7	9	2	8	

WEST SCORECARD:

HOLE	1	2	3	4	5	6	7	8	9	TOTAL
REG.	397	380	196	356	137	490	131	500	420	3,007
SHORT	378	362	171	339	111	471	105	483	402	2,822
PAR	4	4	3	4	3	5	3	5	4	35
HDCP	3	6	5	7	9	1	8	2	4	

RATES: Weekdays: $17 for 18, $9.50 after 4 p.m. and for 9. Weekends: $20 for 18, $10.50 after 4 p.m. and for 9. Resident rates available. Carts: $19 for 18, $11 for 9.

FACILITIES: Putting green, driving range, golf lessons, pro shop, restaurant, snack shop, bar, banquet facilities, locker rooms, club rental, golf equipment sold, tee time recommended, permanent tee time available.

BIG RUN GOLF CLUB
135TH STREET
LOCKPORT, IL 60441
(708)972-1652 OR (815)838-1057

18-Hole Course, 6,654 Yards, Par 72, CDGA rating 72.2

LOCATION: 35 miles southwest of the Loop, 135th Street 2 miles west of Route 171

SEASON: End of March through end of November

GOLF PROFESSIONAL: Stan Vickers

COURSE OWNER: George Gee

GREENS SUPERINTENDENT: Terry Hogan

Big Run Golf Club was built by Muelenford/Sneed and opened in 1930. The 18-hole layout is very challenging with several hundred trees lining the watered fairways. The hilly terrain yields few level lies, and Big Run Creek winds through the course, coming into play on 7 holes. Four lakes and almost 50 bunkers also add to the challenge. An extensive program of design changes and improvements was started in 1980 by Didier Co. and Dick Nugent. Ten holes have been redesigned so far with continual changes affecting all 18 holes planned for the future.

SCORECARD:

HOLE	1	2	3	4	5	6	7	8	9	OUT
REG.	358	406	118	348	515	444	141	378	610	3,318
WOMEN	336	385	107	294	457	427	112	347	600	3,065
PAR	4	4	3	4	5	4	3	4	5	36
HDCP	9	7	17	11	5	3	15	13	1	

HOLE	10	11	12	13	14	15	16	17	18	IN	TOTAL
REG.	312	416	395	185	367	591	167	361	542	3,336	6,654
WOMEN	279	348	388	95	355	564	110	340	535	3,014	6,079
PAR	4	4	4	3	4	5	3	4	5	36	72
HDCP	18	4	10	8	12	2	14	16	6		

RATES: Weekdays: $28, $20 twilight. Weekends: $28, $20 twilight. Carts: $12 per person, $10 per person after 3 p.m. May 30 through September 5, carts required before 3 p.m.

FACILITIES: Putting green, pro shop, restaurant, snack shop, bar, banquet facilities, locker rooms, club rental, golf equipment sold, tee time recommended.

CANTIGNY GOLF
27 WEST 270 MACK ROAD
WHEATON, IL 60187
(708)668-3323

18-Hole Course, 6,709 Yards, Par 72, CDGA rating 72.4
9-Hole Course, 2,497 Yards, Par 36, CDGA rating 35.3
LOCATION: 30 miles northwest of the Loop
SEASON: April through October
GOLF PROFESSIONAL: Bob Jacobs
COURSE OWNER: Cantigny Trust
COURSE MANAGER: Mike Nass

Cantigny Golf's 27 holes were designed by Roger Packard to be enjoyed by golfers of all skill levels. It opened in April 1989 and was nominated "best public course built in 1989" by *Golf Digest*. At 6,709 yards from the back tees, the 18-hole course is long but not overwhelming. There are plenty of hazards to test your accuracy. The course is heavily wooded and has 12 lakes, 1 creek, and 76 bunkers to attract your shots. The greens are small, and the watered fairways offer generous landing areas for your tee shots on most holes. Cantigny is a beautiful facility with no permanent tee times, no leagues, and few outings, making it easier to reserve a tee time.

SCORECARD:

HOLE	1	2	3	4	5	6	7	8	9	OUT
GOLD	344	474	119	288	308	354	423	103	322	2,735
RED	375	499	183	320	358	413	490	140	389	3,167
WHITE	405	539	200	363	374	440	516	165	420	3,422
PAR	4	5	3	4	4	4	5	3	4	36
HDCP	17	1	13	15	11	3	9	7	5	

HOLE	10	11	12	13	14	15	16	17	18	IN	TOTAL
GOLD	321	479	310	125	432	280	305	139	295	2,686	5,421
RED	370	532	348	171	491	324	369	154	341	3,100	6,267
WHITE	395	556	370	191	516	335	388	171	365	3,287	6,709
PAR	4	5	4	3	5	4	4	3	4	36	72
HDCP	10	2	14	8	12	18	6	16	4		

HOLE	19	20	21	22	23	24	25	26	27	TOTAL
GOLD	314	408	284	281	106	268	425	120	291	2,497
RED	388	478	332	351	126	344	487	171	370	3,047
WHITE	406	509	374	366	151	365	507	183	392	3,253
PAR	4	5	4	4	3	4	5	3	4	36
HDCP	7	2	8	5	9	1	4	6	3	

RATES: Open Tuesday through Sunday: $45 for 18 walking, $55 with cart; $19 for 9 walking, $24 with cart.

FACILITIES: Putting green, driving range, golf lessons, pro shop, restaurant, snack shop, bar, banquet facilities, locker rooms, club rental, golf equipment sold, tee time recommended.

CARRIAGE GREENS COUNTRY CLUB
8700 CARRIAGE GREENS DRIVE
DARIEN, IL 60525
(708)985-3730

18-Hole Course, 6,451 Yards, Par 70, CDGA rating 70.1
LOCATION: 25 miles southwest of Chicago
SEASON: Open all year until the first snow
DIRECTOR OF GOLF: Lou Zegaldo
COURSE OWNER: Dennis Broderick
GREENS SUPERINTENDENT: Phil Bersin

Carriage Greens is a beautiful golf course surrounded by homes and trees, featuring mostly flat terrain and tight to wide-open, watered fairways. The course is heavily wooded, and there are 72 sand traps, making accuracy an important factor if you want to score well here. The big hitter will find this a challenging course, but the weekend golfer will enjoy playing here as well.

SCORECARD:

HOLE	1	2	3	4	5	6	7	8	9	OUT
WHITE	331	380	143	515	385	174	382	396	370	3,076
RED	321	370	143	500	360	164	302	371	350	2,881
PAR	4	4	3	5	4	3	4	4	4	35
HDCP	16	8	18	12	6	14	4	2	10	

HOLE	10	11	12	13	14	15	16	17	18	IN	TOTAL
WHITE	359	143	441	539	180	466	390	456	401	3,375	6,451
RED	349	121	391	529	180	456	380	441	261	3,108	5,989
PAR	4	3	4	5	3	4	4	4	4	35	70
HDCP	15	17	7	13	11	1	9	3	5		

RATES: Weekdays: $22 for 18, $25 includes cart before 9 a.m and after 3 p.m. Weekends: $36 includes cart which is mandatory. $15 after 4 p.m. every day. Carts: $24.
FACILITIES: Putting green, golf lessons, pro shop, restaurant, snack shop, bar, banquet facilities, locker rooms, club rental, golf equipment sold, cart required, tee time recommended, permanent tee time available.

COG HILL GOLF AND COUNTRY CLUB
119TH STREET AND ARCHER AVENUE
LEMONT, IL 60439
(708)257-5872 OR (312)242-1717

Number 1: 18-Hole Course, 6,224 Yards, Par 71, CDGA rating 69.2
Number 2: 18-Hole Course, 6,240 Yards, Par 72, CDGA rating 69.4
Number 3: 18-Hole Course, 6,298 Yards, Par 72, CDGA rating 69.5
Number 4: 18-Hole Course, 6,992 Yards, Par 72, CDGA rating 75.4
LOCATION: 20 miles southwest of Chicago
SEASON: Open all year
COURSE OWNER: Joe Jemsek
GREENS SUPERINTENDENT: Ken Lapp

Located 20 miles southwest of the Loop, Cog Hill is every golfer's dream. Four 18-hole championship courses are situated on over 1,000 acres of gently rolling terrain. Numbers 1 and 3 are open layouts with beautiful mature trees lining many of the fairways. Number 2 is tighter and heavily wooded with large rolling greens.

Number 4, Dubsdread, is rated by *Golf Digest* as one of the country's toughest courses. Designed by Dick Wilson and Joe Lee, Dubsdread has long narrow fairways, more than 100 traps, and many large trees to test your accuracy. The greens range from small to large, and many are elevated. Trap placement around the greens requires the golfer to hit high, soft approach shots. Dubsdread is the ideal course for the player with confidence.

NUMBER 1 COURSE SCORECARD:

HOLE	1	2	3	4	5	6	7	8	9	OUT
WHITE	549	375	391	142	312	471	411	210	410	3,271
RED	465	383	382	130	300	464	314	177	400	3,015
PAR	5	4	4	3	4	5	4	3	4	36
HDCP	1	11	8	18	13	3	9	15	5	

HOLE	10	11	12	13	14	15	16	17	18	IN	TOTAL
WHITE	169	376	325	473	310	392	419	177	312	2,953	6,224
RED	146	347	298	455	256	365	384	155	299	2,705	5,720
PAR	3	4	4	5	4	4	4	3	4	35	71
HDCP	17	6	10	2	14	7	4	16	12		

NUMBER 2 COURSE SCORECARD:

HOLE	1	2	3	4	5	6	7	8	9	OUT
BLUE	311	366	540	152	460	384	385	499	294	3,391
WHITE	311	366	508	128	460	350	385	471	294	3,273
RED	291	346	493	120	450	319	371	446	287	3,123
PAR	4	4	5	3	5	4	4	5	4	38
HDCP	13	9	4	17	3	11	7	1	15	

HOLE	10	11	12	13	14	15	16	17	18	IN	TOTAL
BLUE	320	364	320	135	454	371	297	402	186	2,849	6,240
WHITE	320	364	320	135	409	371	287	402	160	2,768	6,041
RED	309	358	282	122	401	355	269	386	150	2,632	5,755
PAR	4	4	4	3	4	4	4	4	3	34	72
HDCP	8	6	10	18	2	12	14	5	16		

NUMBER 3 COURSE SCORECARD:

HOLE	1	2	3	4	5	6	7	8	9	OUT
WHITE	255	353	513	127	365	271	344	383	176	2,787
RED	245	340	440	110	350	255	322	370	162	2,594
PAR	4	4	5	3	4	4	4	4	3	35
HDCP	14	10	2	18	6	12	8	4	16	

HOLE	10	11	12	13	14	15	16	17	18	IN	TOTAL
WHITE	345	583	166	394	397	492	201	529	404	3,511	6,298
RED	266	454	111	382	267	425	184	384	318	2,791	5,385
PAR	4	5	3	4	4	5	3	5	4	37	72
HDCP	13	1	17	11	9	5	15	3	7		

NUMBER 4 COURSE SCORECARD:

HOLE	1	2	3	4	5	6	7	8	9	OUT
BLUE	446	170	398	407	519	226	411	368	575	3,520
WHITE	412	143	358	358	478	192	372	326	549	3,188
RED	388	137	353	334	470	144	285	320	459	2,890
PAR	4	3	4	4	5	3	4	4	5	36
HDCP	7	17	11	5	9	15	3	13	1	

HOLE	10	11	12	13	14	15	16	17	18	IN	TOTAL
BLUE	362	517	206	446	197	498	397	401	448	3,472	6,992
WHITE	329	498	180	381	184	456	374	380	396	3,178	6,366
RED	316	495	149	354	178	423	363	341	365	2,984	5,874
PAR	4	5	3	4	3	5	4	4	4	36	72
HDCP	14	8	18	2	16	6	10	12	4		

RATES: Weekdays: Courses 1 and 3: $23, $12.50 after 3 p.m., $8 after 6 p.m. Course 2: $27, $15 after 3 p.m. Course 4: $65 includes cart. Weekends: Courses 1 and 3: $27, $15 after 3 p.m., $11 after 4:30 p.m., $8 after 6 p.m. Course 2: $30, $16 after 3 p.m. Course 4: $65 for 18 includes cart. Carts: $23, $16 for twilight. $1 discount for cash. VISA, Mastercard, Discover accepted.

FACILITIES: Putting green, driving range, golf lessons, pro shop, restaurant, snack shop, bar, banquet facilities, locker rooms, club rental, golf equipment sold, foursomes only on weekends, tee time recommended, permanent tee time available after noon.

COUNTRY LAKES COUNTRY CLUB
5 SOUTH 100 FAIRWAY DRIVE
NAPERVILLE, IL 60540
(708)420-1060

18-Hole Course, 6,554 Yards, Par 73, CDGA rating 70.5
LOCATION: 25 miles west of the Loop
SEASON: Early spring through fall
GOLF PROFESSIONAL: Ken Kaulen
DIRECTOR OF GOLF: Lou Zegaldo
COURSE OWNER: Robert Krilich
GREENS SUPERINTENDENT: Lee Schneiders

Built in 1973 with 3 sets of tees, this 18-hole layout offers a fair test for golfers of all skill levels. The watered fairways offer generous landing areas for most of your tee shots, and water comes into play on 9 holes. The course is flat with scattered concentrations of small- to medium-sized trees. The club's golf pro, Ken Kaulen, set the course record with a score of 67.

SCORECARD:

HOLE	1	2	3	4	5	6	7	8	9	OUT
BLUE	486	391	399	197	489	445	355	373	192	3,327
WHITE	471	376	384	182	479	430	340	358	177	3,197
RED	415	355	361	154	469	378	320	310	145	2,907
PAR	5	4	4	3	5	4	4	4	3	36
HDCP	5	13	11	15	7	1	9	3	17	

HOLE	10	11	12	13	14	15	16	17	18	IN	TOTAL
BLUE	355	494	400	174	403	517	514	207	454	3,518	6,845
WHITE	340	479	385	159	388	502	499	166	439	3,357	6,554
RED	315	434	364	129	369	483	480	105	406	3,115	6,022
PAR	4	5	4	3	4	5	5	3	4	37	73
HDCP	14	12	2	18	8	6	10	16	4		

RATES: Weekdays: $18 for 18, $12 after 4 p.m. and for 9. Weekends: $22 for 18, $14 after 4 p.m. and for 9. Resident rates available. Carts: $22 for 18, $11 for 9.

FACILITIES: Putting green, driving range, golf lessons, pro shop, restaurant, snack shop, bar, banquet facilities, locker rooms, club rental, golf equipment sold, cart required, tee time recommended, permanent tee time available.

DOWNERS GROVE GOLF CLUB
2420 HADDOW AVENUE
DOWNERS GROVE, IL 60515
(708)963-1306

9-Hole Course, 2,746 Yards, Par 34, CDGA rating 66.3
LOCATION: 25 miles west of Chicago
SEASON: March through November
GOLF PROFESSIONAL: Bob Nelson
COURSE OWNER: Downers Grove Park District
GREENS SUPERINTENDENT: Dick Tuttle

Designed by Charles Blair MacDonald, this 9-hole park district course was built in 1892 as an 18-hole course. The fairways are watered, wide open, and gently rolling. There are 14 traps and 3 water hazards to keep the game interesting on this well-maintained layout designed for the average golfer.

SCORECARD:

HOLE	1	2	3	4	5	6	7	8	9	TOTAL
BLUE	419	418	213	183	365	283	389	201	504	2,975
WHITE	411	406	173	180	325	238	375	198	440	2,746
RED	397	379	136	174	315	226	339	178	402	2,546
PAR	4	4	3	3	4	4	4	3	5	34
HDCP	2	1	5	6	7	9	3	4	8	

RATES: Weekdays: $8.75, $8.25 for replays. Weekends: $9.75, $9.25 for replays. Carts: weekdays, $10; weekends, $11.
FACILITIES: Putting green, practice range, golf lessons, pro shop, snack shop, club rental, golf equipment sold.

EVERGREEN COUNTRY CLUB
9100 SOUTH WESTERN AVENUE
EVERGREEN PARK, IL 60642
(312)238-6680

18-hole course, 6,355 yards, Par 71, CDGA Rating 70.02
LOCATION: 91st and Western Avenue
SEASON: Open all year
GREENS SUPERINTENDENT: John Clark

Evergreen is a course with a detailed landscape that appears deceptively short. Reachable greens are guarded by shallow bunkers that put a premium on accurate short irons or a soft touch from the sand. Very large trees line many of the narrow fairways, requiring a straight tee shot to avoid trouble. The holes vary in length and look, with some rolling fairways providing difficult lies and an occasional blind shot. Accurate tee shots are rewarded, as the ball sits up on watered, bentgrass fairways and bunkers are few. The course has several elevated tees and greens, although never on the same hole. Evergreen is a classically styled course that has remained essentially unchanged since its opening in 1921. Here you will have the opportunity to make use of all your clubs in a variety of shots. Conveniently located for golfers with limited travel time, Evergreen has an appropriate motto: "Play golf as near as your backyard."

SCORECARD:

HOLE	1	2	3	4	5	6	7	8	9	OUT
YARDS	402	375	148	408	476	520	396	341	220	3,286
PAR	4	4	3	4	5	5	4	4	3	36
HDCP	8	11	17	6	3	2	7	12	15	

HOLE	10	11	12	13	14	15	16	17	18	IN	TOTAL
YARDS	295	348	146	546	422	420	115	395	362	3,049	6,355
PAR	4	4	3	5	4	4	3	4	4	35	71
HDCP	14	13	16	1	5	4	18	9	10		

RATES: Weekdays: $16 before 8:45 a.m., $19 after 8:45 a.m., $11 after 3 p.m. Weekends: $23, $12 after 3 p.m. Carts: $22.
FACILITIES: Putting green, pro shop, snack shop, bar, locker rooms, club rental, golf equipment sold.

FOX BEND GOLF COURSE
ROUTE 34
OSWEGO, IL 60543
(708)554-3939

18-Hole Course, 6,360 Yards, Par 71, CDGA rating N/A
LOCATION: 9 miles west of Route 59 on U.S. 34
SEASON: April through November
GOLF PROFESSIONAL: Leon McNair
COURSE OWNER: Oswegoland and Fox Valley Park Districts
GREENS SUPERINTENDENT: Jim McNair

Fox Bend is ranked as one of the top 10 public courses in the Chicago area by the *Chicago Tribune* and *Chicago Sun-Times*. Built by the Wadsworth Golf Construction Company on gently rolling hills, scenic Fox Bend opened to the public in June 1967. Five 400-yard par 4s and plenty of water and sand will make you use every club in your bag to reach the large, rolling greens. This well-designed course plays longer than the 6,660 yards shown on the scorecard.

SCORECARD:

HOLE	1	2	3	4	5	6	7	8	9	OUT
BLUE	345	205	375	425	490	200	525	405	420	3,390
YELLOW	330	185	350	405	480	170	515	395	410	3,240
RED	315	165	325	335	440	130	475	385	400	2,970
PAR	4	3	4	4	5	3	5	4	4	36
HDCP	15	17	9	1	3	13	11	7	5	

HOLE	10	11	12	13	14	15	16	17	18	IN	TOTAL
BLUE	165	505	380	170	430	390	450	235	545	3,270	6,660
YELLOW	150	490	360	160	415	380	430	210	525	3,120	6,360
RED	140	440	340	145	400	370	410	185	500	2,930	5,900
PAR	3	5	4	3	4	4	4	3	5	35	71
HDCP	18	14	12	16	2	8	4	10	6		

RATES: Weekdays: $20 for 18, $12 for 9. Weekends: $24 for 18, $20 after 2 p.m., $14 after 4 p.m. Resident rates available. Carts: $22 for 18, $13 for 9.

FACILITIES: Putting green, driving range, golf lessons, pro shop, restaurant, bar, banquet facilities, locker rooms, club rental, golf equipment sold, fivesomes allowed, tee time required.

FRESH MEADOW GOLF AND COUNTRY CLUB
2144 SOUTH WOLF ROAD
HILLSIDE, IL 60162
(708)449-3434

18-Hole Course, 6,178 Yards, Par 70, CDGA rating 69.1
LOCATION: 30 minutes from the Loop, Eisenhower to Wolf Road
SEASON: Open all year
GOLF PROFESSIONAL: Mike Mishack
COURSE OWNER: American Golf Corporation
GREENS SUPERINTENDENT: Jim Foster

American Golf Corporation purchased this course from Joe Jemsek in December 1988. Fresh Meadow is very manageable for the average player. Water is in play on 4 holes, and the large greens are well bunkered. The watered fairways are flat, and several are lined with trees ranging in size from small to large. The course is always in very good condition and is easily accessible from the Tri-State tollway and Eisenhower expressway.

SCORECARD:

HOLE	1	2	3	4	5	6	7	8	9	OUT
REG.	437	132	464	428	168	175	454	374	366	2,998
WOMEN	368	101	444	413	138	155	439	351	346	2,755
PAR	4	3	5	4	3	3	5	4	4	35
HDCP	2	18	4	8	14	16	6	12	10	

HOLE	10	11	12	13	14	15	16	17	18	IN	TOTAL
REG.	443	361	208	138	320	459	446	399	406	3,180	6,178
WOMEN	417	323	170	118	307	445	432	387	389	2,988	5,743
PAR	4	4	3	3	4	5	4	4	4	35	70
HDCP	3	13	15	17	11	5	1	9	7		

RATES: Weekdays: $21 for 18, $14 for 9, $13 after 6 p.m. Weekends: $24 for 18 (foursomes required before 12 p.m.), $15 for 9, $13 after 6 p.m. Carts: $22 for 18, $14 for 9.
FACILITIES: Putting green, driving range, golf lessons, pro shop, restaurant, snack shop, bar, locker rooms, club rental, golf equipment sold, fivesomes allowed, tee time recommended, permanent tee time available.

GLENDALE GOLF CLUB
5 NORTH 181 GLEN ELLYN ROAD
BLOOMINGDALE, IL 60108
(708)529-6232

18-Hole Course, 6,317 Yards, Par 72, CDGA rating 69.6

LOCATION: 25 miles west of the Loop, Lake Street and Glen Ellyn Road

SEASON: April through November

DIRECTOR OF GOLF: Don Helmig

COURSE OWNER: Hamilton Partners, Inc.

GREENS SUPERINTENDENT: Paul Schaeffer

Glendale is a short, straight, par-72 layout with very little sand and only 1 water hazard. The fairways are wide open and mostly flat, and the large greens are not bunkered. Trees create most of the trouble you'll encounter on this established Chicago-area course that the high handicapper will enjoy.

SCORECARD:

HOLE	1	2	3	4	5	6	7	8	9	OUT
YARDS	491	437	343	411	370	175	379	475	186	3,267
PAR	5	4	4	4	4	3	4	5	3	36
HDCP	5	2	11	3	10	16	9	7	15	

HOLE	10	11	12	13	14	15	16	17	18	IN	TOTAL
YARDS	317	364	314	132	410	326	165	444	501	2,973	6,240
PAR	4	4	4	3	4	4	3	5	5	36	72
HDCP	12	1	14	18	4	13	17	8	6		

RATES: Weekdays: $18.50 for 18, $11.50 after 4 p.m. and for 9. Seniors: $12.50 for 18, $8.50 for 9. Weekends: $20.50 for 18, $13.50 for 9 after 2 p.m., $11.50 after 4 p.m. Carts: $20 for 18, $14 for 9.

FACILITIES: Putting green, pro shop, snack shop, bar, banquet facilities, locker rooms, club rental, golf equipment sold, tee time recommended, permanent tee time available.

GLENDALE LAKES GOLF COURSE
1550 President Street
Glendale Heights, IL 60139
(708)260-0018

18-Hole Course, 5,870 Yards, Par 71, CDGA rating 69.1
LOCATION: 15 miles southwest of O'Hare
SEASON: March 15 through November 30
GOLF PROFESSIONAL: Bill Krueger
COURSE OWNER: Village of Glendale Heights
GREENS SUPERINTENDENT: Paul Knulty

Glendale Lakes is a course all golfers will enjoy playing with its flat terrain and few trees, but the 7 ponds and 1 large lake call for steady target golf. The watered fairways are bent grass, and the greens are large and well trapped. Designed by Dick Nugent and built in 1987, this course has a slope rating of 121.

SCORECARD:

HOLE	1	2	3	4	5	6	7	8	9	OUT
BLUE	366	503	174	286	398	128	498	177	414	2,944
WHITE	345	491	163	273	386	110	479	162	394	2,803
RED	315	473	127	201	368	84	451	139	365	2,523
PAR	4	5	3	4	4	3	5	3	4	35
HDCP	9	1	15	11	5	17	3	13	7	

HOLE	10	11	12	13	14	15	16	17	18	IN	TOTAL
BLUE	507	406	386	385	377	157	161	303	517	3,199	6,143
WHITE	493	393	373	371	363	141	148	287	498	3,067	5,870
RED	471	373	353	349	342	117	128	263	471	2,867	5,390
PAR	5	4	4	4	4	3	3	4	5	36	71
HDCP	4	6	8	10	12	16	18	14	2		

RATES: Weekdays: $19 for 18; $12 for 9; $13 after 4 p.m.; $10 after 6 p.m.; seniors and juniors, $13. Weekends: $22 for 18; $14 for 9 (9-hole golf after 12 p.m. only); $12 after 4 p.m. Resident rates available. Carts: $22 for 18, $12 for 9.

FACILITIES: Putting green, golf lessons, pro shop, restaurant, snack shop, bar, banquet facilities, locker rooms, club rental, golf equipment sold, fivesomes allowed, tee time recommended, permanent tee time available.

GLENEAGLES COUNTRY CLUB
123RD AND BELL ROAD
LEMONT, IL 60439
(708)257-5466

White: 18-Hole Course, 6,080 Yards, Par 70, CDGA rating 68.6
Red: 18-Hole Course, 6,090 Yards, Par 70, CDGA rating 67.5
LOCATION: 4 miles west of LaGrange Road on 123rd Street
SEASON: March until December
DIRECTOR OF GOLF: Bob Scharbert
COURSE OWNER: Ed McNulty
GREENS SUPERINTENDENT: Keith Fuchs

Gleneagles has two 18-hole courses with watered, well-manicured fairways and greens. Both courses are fairly wide open with large trees lining the fairways. The best hole on the Red Course is the 465-yard 17th. Your first shot has to be hit long and straight, because there are out-of-bounds limits on the left side and a large willow tree on the right. The second shot has to be lifted over a large pond to a well-trapped, medium-sized green. The terrain varies from flat to hilly and both courses play longer than the scorecards indicate because there are several long par 4s. There is only 1 water hazard (the pond on the 17th hole on the Red Course), but the traps surrounding the greens and the clusters of mature trees provide plenty of challenge for golfers of all skill levels.

WHITE COURSE SCORECARD:

HOLE	1	2	3	4	5	6	7	8	9	OUT
YARDS	340	155	450	410	360	365	165	275	510	3,030
PAR	4	3	4	4	4	4	3	4	5	35
HDCP	15	9	1	3	5	13	11	17	7	

HOLE	10	11	12	13	14	15	16	17	18	IN	TOTAL
YARDS	400	330	200	450	350	375	350	200	345	3,050	6,080
PAR	4	4	3	5	4	4	4	3	4	35	70
HDCP	4	18	8	6	12	2	14	16	10		

RED COURSE SCORECARD:

HOLE	1	2	3	4	5	6	7	8	9	OUT
YARDS	330	415	375	440	375	150	425	200	270	2,980
PAR	4	4	4	4	4	3	4	3	4	34
HDCP	9	5	11	3	7	15	1	13	17	

HOLE	10	11	12	13	14	15	16	17	18	IN	TOTAL
YARDS	490	510	165	325	200	500	125	465	330	3,110	6,090
PAR	5	5	3	4	3	5	3	4	4	36	70
HDCP	8	4	16	12	14	6	18	2	10		

RATES: Weekdays: $21; $12 after 3 p.m.; seniors, $20. Weekends: $26, $14 after 3 p.m. Carts: $22, $15 for single riders.

FACILITIES: Three putting greens, golf lessons, pro shop, restaurant, snack shop, bar, locker rooms, club rental, golf equipment sold, tee time required on weekends, tee time recommended, permanent tee time available.

HICKORY CREEK GOLF COURSE AND DRIVING RANGE
200 Saint Francis Road
Frankfort, IL 60423
(815)469-1717

9-Hole Course, 1,811 Yards, Par 30, CDGA rating N/A
LOCATION: 1½ miles from I-80, Harlem South exit
SEASON: April 1 through November 15
GOLF PROFESSIONAL: Ken Malnar
COURSE OWNER: Henry J. Olivieri, Sr.
GREENS SUPERINTENDENT: Greg Fagiano

Hickory Creek has a short 9-hole layout with narrow fairways and small elevated greens. Although the course is only about 1,800 yards long, water comes into play on 4 holes, and a fenceline marks the boundaries on 5 holes, making accuracy a must. The 3rd hole is a tough 195-yard par 3 bordered by water on the right and out-of-bounds on the left. The elevated green is small and difficult to hold. Hickory Creek also features a large, lighted driving range with grass tees.

SCORECARD:

HOLE	1	2	3	4	5	6	7	8	9	TOTAL
BLUE	362	116	195	137	221	360	145	154	121	1,811
WHITE	356	110	190	132	216	348	140	151	116	1,759
RED	330	108	180	128	216	328	140	150	116	1,696
PAR	4	3	3	3	4	4	3	3	3	30
HDCP	1	9	4	6	3	2	5	7	8	

RATES: Weekdays: $14 for 18; $7.50 for 9; senior citizens, $6 until 2 p.m.; juniors, $5 on Tuesdays. Weekends: $18 for 18, $9.50 for 9.
Carts: weekdays, $7; senior citizens, $6 until 2 p.m.; weekends, $9.
FACILITIES: Putting green, driving range, golf lessons, club rental, permanent tee time available.

INDIAN LAKES RESORT
250 WEST SCHICK ROAD
BLOOMINGDALE, IL 60108
(708)529-0200 OR (708)529-6466

Iroquois Trail: 18-Hole Course, 6,580 Yards, Par 72, CDGA rating 70.9
Sioux Trail: 18-Hole Course, 6,564 Yards, Par 72, CDGA rating 71.1
LOCATION: 35 miles west of the Loop
SEASON: March 15 through November 15
GOLF PROFESSIONAL: Brian Ihnat
COURSE OWNER: VMS Realty
GREENS SUPERINTENDENT: Gene Thompson

    Indian Lakes has two 18-hole courses, Sioux Trail and Iroquois Trail. Built in 1962 and designed by Robert Bruce Harris, the resort was purchased from Carson, Pirie, Scott and Co. in 1984 by VMS Realty, the current owner. Sioux Trail is the more difficult layout, with water coming into play on several holes. Although the course has few trees and the terrain is flat, both layouts have many large, well-placed traps, and the greens are well bunkered, making accuracy a must. You want to hit high soft approach shots. Both Indian Lakes courses provide enjoyable and challenging golf for every level of player.

IROQUOIS TRAIL SCORECARD:

HOLE	1	2	3	4	5	6	7	8	9	OUT
WHITE	413	528	377	172	348	511	155	359	438	3,301
RED	391	509	357	153	329	493	137	340	418	3,127
PAR	4	5	4	3	4	5	3	4	4	36
HDCP	7	1	9	15	13	3	17	11	5	

HOLE	10	11	12	13	14	15	16	17	18	IN	TOTAL
WHITE	427	551	388	179	366	491	335	141	401	3,279	6,580
RED	406	533	368	156	345	477	316	122	388	3,111	6,238
PAR	4	5	4	3	4	5	4	3	4	36	72
HDCP	6	2	10	16	12	4	14	18	8		

SIOUX TRAIL SCORECARD:

HOLE	1	2	3	4	5	6	7	8	9	OUT
WHITE	409	479	383	139	330	546	171	395	427	3,279
RED	393	459	363	124	313	528	152	375	407	3,114
PAR	4	5	4	3	4	5	3	4	4	36
HDCP	7	3	9	17	13	1	15	11	5	

HOLE	11	10	12	13	14	15	16	17	18	IN	TOTAL
WHITE	409	496	365	184	520	386	346	152	427	3,285	6,564
RED	383	476	346	167	500	366	328	135	410	3,111	6,225
PAR	4	5	4	3	5	4	4	3	4	36	72
HDCP	8	4	12	16	2	10	14	18	6		

RATES: Weekdays: $38 includes cart required before 4 p.m.; after 4 p.m., $27 with cart, $16 walking. Weekends: $42 includes cart; after 4 p.m., $27 with cart, $16 walking.

FACILITIES: Putting green, golf lessons, pro shop, restaurant, snack shop, bar, banquet facilities, locker rooms, club rental, golf equipment sold, cart required until 4 p.m. daily, tee time required.

INWOOD GOLF COURSE
3000 WEST JEFFERSON STREET
JOLIET, IL 60435
(815)741-7265

18-Hole Course, 6,078 Yards, Par 71, CDGA rating 69.4
LOCATION: 2½ miles east of Route 55 on Route 52
SEASON: March through November
COURSE OWNER: Joliet Park District
GREENS SUPERINTENDENT: Jim Hall

Playing Inwood is almost like playing two different courses. The front 9 has small, slow greens with few bunkers and measures only 2,959 yards. A creek winds through this part of the course, coming into play on 5 holes. The back 9 is longer with 3,229 yards, bent-grass fairways, and large well-bunkered, undulating greens. Lakes factor into play on 5 of the final 9 holes. Although the course is not very long, the narrow fairways, water, and bunkers keep scores fairly high.

SCORECARD:

HOLE	1	2	3	4	5	6	7	8	9	OUT
BLUE	185	500	168	541	173	396	352	353	291	2,959
WHITE	185	500	168	541	173	396	352	353	291	2,959
RED	177	480	148	470	162	281	266	325	285	2,594
PAR	3	5	3	5	3	4	4	4	4	35
HDCP	11	3	15	1	13	5	7	9	17	

HOLE	10	11	12	13	14	15	16	17	18	IN	TOTAL
BLUE	414	330	521	184	397	361	146	509	367	3,229	6,188
WHITE	404	319	511	167	385	351	133	495	354	3,119	6,078
RED	394	308	501	155	373	341	120	483	341	3,016	5,610
PAR	4	4	5	3	4	4	3	5	4	36	71
HDCP	6	8	2	16	10	12	18	4	14		

RATES: Weekdays: resident: $9 for 18, $7.50 for 9; nonresident: $16 for 18, $11 for 9. Weekends: resident: $11 for 18, $9 for 9; nonresident: $19 for 18, $13 for 9. Carts: $16 for 18, $9 for 9.
FACILITIES: Putting green, driving range, golf lessons, pro shop, snack shop, bar, club rental, golf equipment sold.

NAPERBROOK GOLF COURSE
111TH STREET AND PLAINFIELD ROAD
NAPERVILLE, IL 60540
(708)378-4215

18-Hole Course, 6,400 Yards, Par 72, CDGA rating N/A
LOCATION: 27 miles southwest of the Loop
SEASON: April until November
GOLF PROFESSIONAL: Ed Provow
COURSE OWNER: Naperville Park District
GREENS SUPERINTENDENT: Bob Surufka

Naperbrook is a new course that opened in late 1990. Designed by Roger Packard, it is a refreshing retreat from residential-type courses. The course is relatively flat and wide open with a plan to begin planting a variety of trees. Naperbrook can play at more than 6,700 yards and challenge golfers of all levels. There are 45 sand traps, located primarily around the large, undulating greens, and 12 water hazards come into play on 10 holes.

SCORECARD:

HOLE	1	2	3	4	5	6	7	8	9	OUT
GOLD	400	360	540	180	410	420	530	190	375	3,405
BLUE	380	340	520	160	390	400	505	170	355	3,220
WHITE	355	315	495	135	365	375	480	145	330	2,995
RED	315	275	455	115	325	335	430	125	290	2,665
PAR	4	4	5	3	4	4	5	3	4	36

HOLE	10	11	12	13	14	15	16	17	18	IN	TOTAL
GOLD	355	365	165	405	580	210	385	395	515	3,375	6,780
BLUE	335	360	140	385	540	185	365	375	495	3,180	6,400
WHITE	310	335	125	360	520	160	340	350	475	2,975	5,970
RED	270	295	105	320	470	135	300	310	415	2,620	5,285
PAR	4	4	3	4	5	3	4	4	5	36	72

RATES: Weekdays: $18 for 18; $13 twilight and for 9; seniors, $14; juniors, $10. Weekends: $25 for 18, $14 twilight. Carts $18 for 18, $12 for 9.

FACILITIES: Putting green, driving range, golf lessons, pro shop, snack shop, bar, club rental, golf equipment sold, tee time recommended.

NORDIC HILLS RESORT
ROUTE 53 AND NORDIC ROAD
ITASCA, IL 60143
(708)773-2750

18-Hole Course, 5,853 Yards, Par 71, CDGA rating 68.9
LOCATION: 25 miles west of the Loop
SEASON: April through November
GOLF PROFESSIONAL: Mike Wallner
COURSE OWNER: Bergner's
GREENS SUPERINTENDENT: Rick Sikora and Gene Thompson

Nordic Hills is heavily wooded with tight fairways. The front 9 features hilly terrain, while the back 9 is mostly flat. Greens are elevated, and grass bunkers make it difficult to pitch and run onto the putting surfaces. Water in the form of a stream and a lake comes into play on the 6th, 7th, 10th, and 11th holes, but there are few sand traps to worry about. The excellent facilities include restaurants, meeting rooms, and hotel accommodations, making this a popular facility for corporate outings.

SCORECARD:

HOLE	1	2	3	4	5	6	7	8	9	OUT
YARDS	363	337	356	317	255	164	476	195	275	2,738
PAR	4	4	4	4	4	3	5	3	4	35
HDCP	11	13	9	14	15	12	16	6	17	

HOLE	10	11	12	13	14	15	16	17	18	IN	TOTAL
YARDS	547	197	515	94	349	243	282	411	477	3,115	5,853
PAR	5	3	5	3	4	3	4	4	5	36	71
HDCP	4	5	2	18	10	1	8	3	7		

RATES: Weekdays: $30 before 8 a.m., $38 after 8 a.m. includes cart which is mandatory, $16 walking after 4 p.m. Weekends: $42 includes cart, $16 walking after 4 p.m.
FACILITIES: Putting green, golf lessons, pro shop, restaurant, snack shop, bar, banquet facilities, locker rooms, club rental, golf equipment sold, cart required, tee time recommended.

OAK BROOK HILLS
3500 MIDWEST ROAD
OAK BROOK, IL 60522
(708)850-5555

18-Hole Course, 6,409 Yards, Par 70, CDGA rating 70.3
LOCATION: 25 miles west of the Loop
SEASON: April through November
GOLF PROFESSIONAL: Randy Bolstad

Oak Brook Hills is a target golf course with beach-type bunkers and bent-grass fairways. Dick Nugent designed the course, which opened in 1986 and has been the site of the BMW Golf Classic and the Ernie Banks March of Dimes Tournament. Built on hilly land and measuring 6,409 yards from the back tees, the course has 11 water holes and 45 sand traps, making shot placement all-important. In addition to the golf course, Oak Brook Hills features 3 restaurants, 3 lounges, 5 tennis courts, meeting rooms, banquet facilities, a complete health and fitness center, and a 400-room hotel.

SCORECARD:

HOLE	1	2	3	4	5	6	7	8	9	OUT
CHAMP.	415	592	520	145	365	185	395	424	180	3,221
WHITE	395	550	500	130	325	165	370	396	165	2,996
RED	335	500	445	110	305	140	365	347	145	2,692
PAR	4	5	5	3	4	3	4	4	3	35
HDCP	7	1	3	17	11	13	9	5	15	

HOLE	10	11	12	13	14	15	16	17	18	IN	TOTAL
CHAMP.	425	540	165	390	530	160	360	175	443	3,188	6,409
WHITE	415	515	135	360	525	140	350	160	423	3,023	6,019
RED	345	430	100	335	505	120	295	135	367	2,632	5,324
PAR	4	5	3	4	5	3	4	3	4	35	70
HDCP	8	2	16	10	4	18	12	14	6		

RATES: Weekdays: $42 includes cart which is required, $30 before 8 a.m. and after 3 p.m. Weekends: $45 includes cart which is required, $35 after 3 p.m.
FACILITIES: Putting green, golf lessons, pro shop, restaurant, snack shop, bar, banquet facilities, locker rooms, club rental, golf equipment sold, cart required, tee time recommended.

OAK HILLS COUNTRY CLUB
13248 SOUTH 76TH AVENUE
PALOS HEIGHTS, IL 60463
(708)448-5544

9-Hole Course, 2,756 Yards, Par 34, CDGA rating 33.0
LOCATION: On 131st Street, 4 blocks west of Harlem
GOLF PROFESSIONAL: Allen Parkes
COURSE OWNER: Lakewood Golf
GREENS SUPERINTENDENT: Allen Parkes

Oak Hills is exactly what you'd expect when you hear the name—a course with plenty of mature oak trees and very hilly terrain. The fairways are narrow, and water comes into play on 6 of the 9 holes. The 514-yard 2nd has a pond on the left and out-of-bounds on the right, making it a very tight driving hole. The 4th is a 420-yard par 4 with water on the left and trees on the right. The green is guarded by large bunkers on both sides. The course was first opened in 1977, and the landscape was designed by Roger Packard, a well-known Midwestern golf course architect.

SCORECARD:

HOLE	1	2	3	4	5	6	7	8	9	TOTAL
CHAMP.	160	527	181	441	186	302	146	283	530	2,756
REG.	140	514	161	420	169	292	131	261	510	2,598
WOMEN	130	501	158	395	132	270	120	255	470	2,431
PAR	3	5	3	4	3	4	3	4	5	34
HDCP	6	2	5	1	4	7	9	8	3	

RATES: Weekdays: $18 for 18, $12 for 9, $10 after 4 p.m. Weekends: $20 for 18, $14 for 9, $10 after 4 p.m. Carts: $22 for 18, $12 for 9.
FACILITIES: Putting green, golf lessons, pro shop, club rental, golf equipment sold, tee time recommended.

OAK MEADOWS GOLF COURSE
900 NORTH WOOD DALE ROAD
ADDISON, IL 60101
(708)595-0071 OR (708)595-1800

18-Hole Course, 6,718 Yards, Par 71, CDGA rating 71.9
LOCATION: 25 miles west of the Loop
SEASON: April 1 through December 1
GOLF PROFESSIONAL: Michael Buros
COURSE OWNER: DuPage County Forest Preserve District
GREENS SUPERINTENDENT: Tom DiGuido
   This is a heavily wooded course with narrow, watered fairways. Placement shots are a must here with large, well-bunkered greens, an average of 3 traps per hole, and 10 water hazards. The course is situated on rolling hills and will test the low handicapper, but the average player will enjoy playing here as well. There is an all-grass driving range available. Tee times can be reserved a week in advance by phone.

SCORECARD:

HOLE	1	2	3	4	5	6	7	8	9	OUT
BLUE	386	397	371	160	450	589	410	456	199	3,418
WHITE	369	386	360	145	407	558	387	440	175	3,227
RED	352	375	349	130	391	478	364	424	151	3,014
PAR	4	4	4	3	4	5	4	4	3	35
HDCP	11	9	15	17	1	3	7	5	13	

HOLE	10	11	12	13	14	15	16	17	18	IN	TOTAL
BLUE	332	410	506	363	402	355	129	358	445	3,300	6,718
WHITE	313	392	492	345	385	341	108	338	435	3,149	6,376
RED	294	374	478	269	368	327	87	318	425	2,940	5,954
PAR	4	4	5	4	4	4	3	4	4	36	71
HDCP	14	6	16	8	4	10	18	12	2		

RATES: Weekdays: $25 for 18, $17 after 4 p.m. Weekends: $27 for 18, $17 after 4 p.m. Resident rates available. Carts: $22 for 18, $13 for 9.
FACILITIES: Putting green, driving range, golf lessons, pro shop, snack shop, bar, banquet facilities, locker rooms, club rental, golf equipment sold, cart required on weekends until noon, tee time recommended, permanent tee time available.

OLD OAK COUNTRY CLUB
143RD STREET AND PARKER ROAD
ORLAND PARK, IL 60462
(708)301-3344

18-Hole Course, 6,357 Yards, Par 71, CDGA rating 68.2

LOCATION: 26 miles southwest of the Loop, 5 miles west of LaGrange Road

SEASON: April through November

GOLF PROFESSIONAL: Tony Margala

COURSE OWNER: Justas Lieponis

GREENS SUPERINTENDENT: Peter Lieponis

Old Oak, which opened as the private 18-hole Kinsman Country Club in 1926, had numerous owners over the years until 1968 when the present owner took charge. The course is heavily wooded, and there are a few tight spots through the woods although the fairways are generally wide open. The rough is light, and the greens, which have been enlarged over the years, are fairly well bunkered. Old Oak is a well-conditioned public course designed for the average golfer.

SCORECARD:

HOLE	1	2	3	4	5	6	7	8	9	OUT
BLUE	504	362	433	165	558	210	361	384	316	3,293
RED	475	336	398	150	536	200	340	360	300	3,095
PAR	5	4	4	3	5	3	4	4	4	36
HDCP	9	17	1	11	3	7	13	5	15	

HOLE	10	11	12	13	14	15	16	17	18	IN	TOTAL
BLUE	468	313	162	341	379	296	136	547	422	3,064	6,357
RED	267	287	134	316	360	278	128	527	415	2,712	5,807
PAR	4	4	3	4	4	4	3	5	4	35	71
HDCP	4	10	14	12	2	16	18	8	6		

RATES: Weekdays: $17 for 18; $12 after 3 p.m. and for 9; seniors, $14. Weekends: $24 for 18, $15 after 3 p.m. and for 9. Carts: $16 for 9, $22 for 18.

FACILITIES: Putting green, golf lessons, pro shop, restaurant, snack shop, bar, banquet facilities, locker rooms, club rental, golf equipment sold, tee time required on weekends, permanent tee time available.

81

PALOS COUNTRY CLUB
131ST STREET AND SOUTHWEST HIGHWAY
PALOS PARK, IL 60464
(708)448-6550

Red: 9-Hole Course, 3,152 Yards, Par 36, CDGA rating N/A
White: 9-Hole Course, 3,220 Yards, Par 36, CDGA rating N/A
Blue: 9-Hole Course, 3,321 Yards, Par 36, CDGA rating N/A
LOCATION: 25 miles southwest of the Loop
SEASON: April 1 through December 1
COURSE OWNER: Palos Country Club, Inc.
GREENS SUPERINTENDENT: Scott Armstrong

Palos has three 9-hole courses designed by Charles P. Maddox. Since 1925, it has been a public course and is currently being remodeled with the addition of lakes, traps, and a new sprinkler system. The course is hilly with wide-open fairways and average-sized greens. The average golfer will enjoy playing here, and once the renovation project is completed the condition of the course should improve. Palos Country Club also has excellent banquet facilities available for up to 1,000 people.

RED COURSE SCORECARD:

HOLE	1	2	3	4	5	6	7	8	9	TOTAL
RED	355	386	174	576	351	383	137	475	315	3,152
PAR	4	4	3	5	4	4	3	5	4	36
HDCP	4	14	6	2	8	10	18	12	16	

WHITE COURSE SCORECARD:

HOLE	1	2	3	4	5	6	7	8	9	TOTAL
WHITE	507	190	426	169	325	507	371	378	347	3,220
PAR	5	3	4	3	4	5	4	4	4	36
HDCP	5	15	1	17	11	3	7	13	9	

BLUE COURSE SCORECARD:

HOLE	10	11	12	13	14	15	16	17	18	TOTAL
BLUE	520	151	324	356	362	339	429	212	538	3,231
PAR	5	3	4	4	4	4	4	3	5	36
HDCP	2	18	12	10	8	16	4	14	6	

RATES: Weekdays: $19 for 18; $12 after 3 p.m. and for 9; senior citizens, $15 for 18, $10 for 9. Weekends: $25 for 18, $15 after 3 p.m.; $15 for 9. Carts: weekdays: $18 for 18, $12 for 9; weekends: $22 for 18, $15 for 9.
FACILITIES: Putting green, driving range, golf lessons, pro shop, restaurant, snack shop, bar, banquet facilities, locker rooms, club rental, golf equipment sold, tee time recommended, permanent tee time available.

PAR 3 GOLF CLUB
62ND AND WOLF ROAD
LA GRANGE, IL 60525
(708)246-9848

9-Hole Course, 1,737 Yards, Par 27, CDGA rating N/A
LOCATION: Between Joliet Road and Plainfield Road
SEASON: Mid-March through Thanksgiving Day
GOLF PROFESSIONAL: Tom Mack
COURSE OWNER: Charles Casper
GREENS SUPERINTENDENT: Tom McNamara

Par 3 has a 1,737-yard layout with wide-open fairways, flat terrain, and elevated, medium-sized greens. Although it is best suited to the beginner and high handicapper, it is still challenging to shoot par here, with four holes measuring over 200 yards. There are no water hazards and very few bunkers to catch errant shots, so swing away!

SCORECARD:

HOLE	1	2	3	4	5	6	7	8	9	TOTAL
YARDS	175	220	190	160	205	155	245	137	250	1,737
PAR	3	3	3	3	3	3	3	3	3	27
HDCP	6	3	5	7	4	8	2	9	1	

RATES: Weekdays: $9. Weekends: $10. Carts: pull carts only, $1.
FACILITIES: Putting green, golf lessons, pro shop, snack shop, club rental, golf equipment sold, tee times on a first-come, first-served basis.

PHEASANT RUN RESORT
ROUTE 64 EAST
ST. CHARLES, IL 60174
(708)584-4914

18-Hole Course, 6,315 Yards, Par 71, CDGA rating N/A
LOCATION: 3 miles west of Route 64 and Route 59 intersection
SEASON: April through November
GOLF PROFESSIONAL: Kirk Lundbeck
DIRECTOR OF GOLF Dennis Johnsen
COURSE OWNER: Ed McArdle
GREENS SUPERINTENDENT: Pete Mirkes

Located east of St. Charles, Illinois, Pheasant Run was designed by
Bill Maddox and opened in 1962. Since 1983, trees have been planted,
lakes added, and tees rebuilt, making the course longer and more
pleasing to the eye. Sand traps surrounding the greens defy your efforts
to pitch and roll. High soft approach shots are required to hit the
putting surfaces. The course is not too long, but the trees, water, and
sand provide plenty of hazards. The course is well suited to golfers of
all skill levels.

SCORECARD:

HOLE	1	2	3	4	5	6	7	8	9	OUT
BLUE	543	200	491	217	287	168	376	319	416	3,017
WHITE	533	187	439	200	269	148	369	256	404	2,805
RED	509	168	387	188	243	128	344	211	388	2,566
PAR	5	3	5	3	4	3	4	4	4	35
HDCP	4	14	2	10	18	16	8	12	6	

HOLE	10	11	12	13	14	15	16	17	18	IN	TOTAL
BLUE	350	537	119	338	430	468	505	227	324	3,298	6,315
WHITE	341	520	100	319	406	449	488	219	308	3,150	5,955
RED	312	498	75	291	368	422	466	202	272	2,906	5,472
PAR	4	5	3	4	4	4	5	3	4	36	71
HDCP	9	1	17	11	5	3	7	13	15		

RATES: Every day: $25 for 18, $14 for 9 and after 3:30 p.m. Early bird
special Monday through Friday: $16 before 10:30 a.m. Carts: $11.50 per
person for 18, $6 per person for 9. Half price during early bird special
and after 3:30 p.m.
FACILITIES: Putting green, driving range, golf lessons, pro shop,
restaurant, snack shop, bar, banquet facilities, locker rooms, club rental,
golf equipment sold, tee time recommended, permanent tee time available.

PHILLIPS PARK GOLF COURSE
HILL AVENUE
AURORA, IL 60505
(708)898-7352

18-Hole Course, 5,931 Yards, Par 71, CDGA rating N/A
LOCATION: 30 minutes southwest of Chicago
SEASON: March 15 through November 15
GOLF PROFESSIONAL: Clarke Kleckner
ASSISTANT PROFESSIONAL: Ted Brodeur
COURSE OWNER: City of Aurora
GREENS SUPERINTENDENT: Jeff Swanson

The high handicapper should score well on this short, 18-hole layout. There are no water hazards and only a few sand traps to worry about. The front 9 is very hilly with a variety of trees, while the back 9 is flat and wide open. The pro shop is being remodeled, and an irrigation system was added in 1991. Phillips Park schedules company outings 2 months in advance and hosts league play on Monday, Wednesday, and Thursday after 3:30 p.m. The course record is 62, set in 1963 by Jerry Boedwig.

SCORECARD:

HOLE	1	2	3	4	5	6	7	8	9	OUT
YARDS	498	180	518	222	297	324	365	342	527	3,273
PAR	5	3	5	3	4	4	4	4	5	37
HDCP	10	12	5	4	14	7	6	11	1	

HOLE	10	11	12	13	14	15	16	17	18	IN	TOTAL
YARDS	333	290	312	361	411	331	272	132	216	2,658	5,931
PAR	4	4	4	4	4	4	4	3	3	34	71
HDCP	9	17	16	8	2	13	18	15	3		

RATES: Weekdays: $9 for 18, $4.50 for 9 and after 4 p.m. Weekends: $15 for 18, $5 after 2:30 p.m. Resident rates available. Carts: $15 for 18, $7.50 for 9.
FACILITIES: Putting green, golf lessons, pro shop, snack shop, golf equipment sold, tee time recommended on weekends.

POTTAWATOMIE GOLF COURSE
NORTH 2ND AVENUE
ST. CHARLES, IL 60174
(708)584-8356

9-Hole Course, 3,005 Yards, Par 35, CDGA rating 67.7
LOCATION: On Fox River near Route 64
SEASON: March 1 through December 23
GOLF PROFESSIONAL: Jim Wheeler
COURSE OWNER: St. Charles Park District
GREENS SUPERINTENDENT: John Stephenson

The golf course is located in Pottawatomie Park which has 45 acres of picnic area, a miniature golf course, tennis courts, a baseball field, playgrounds, 2 large outdoor swimming pools, and 2 paddleboats that go up and down the Fox River. Since the course opened in 1939, the basic layout remains unchanged from the original design by Robert Trent Jones. The rebuilding of 8 greens and conventional tree replacement over the years have caused only subtle alterations in the course's appearance. The land varies from flat to gently rolling, and the watered fairways are tree lined but not overly tight. Although the course is only 3,000 yards long, it challenges the scratch golfer and is playable for the high handicapper.

SCORECARD:

HOLE	1	2	3	4	5	6	7	8	9	TOTAL
BLUE	489	330	345	154	378	368	197	325	419	3,005
WHITE	476	318	330	122	296	333	173	313	381	2,742
RED	411	314	326	112	225	321	154	305	378	2,546
PAR	5	4	4	3	4	4	3	4	4	35
HDCP	17	11	7	13	3	5	9	15	1	

RATES: Weekdays: $17 for 18, $8.50 for 9. Weekends: $21 for 18, $10.50 for 9. Resident rates available. Carts: $18 for 18, $9 for 9.
FACILITIES: Putting green, golf lessons, pro shop, snack shop, club rental, golf equipment sold, tee time recommended, permanent tee time available.

PRESTBURY GOLF CLUB
15 WINTHROP NEW ROAD
SUGAR GROVE, IL 60554
(708)466-4177

18-Hole Course, 5,436 Yards, Par 69, CDGA rating 65.1
LOCATION: 20 miles west of Naperville on I-88
SEASON: Open all year
GOLF PROFESSIONAL: Mark Matz
COURSE OWNERS: David Meyer and Joe Foerner
GREENS SUPERINTENDENT: David Meyer

Prestbury was a 9-hole golf course until it was purchased in 1988 by the current owners and reopened in May 1989 as a sporty, 18-hole layout designed for the average player. The terrain is flat, and the narrow fairways lead to small, well-trapped greens. The course is not too long, but water is a factor on 15 of the 18 holes.

SCORECARD:

HOLE	1	2	3	4	5	6	7	8	9	OUT
WHITE	366	387	333	272	354	131	332	138	425	2,738
RED	348	268	295	256	267	111	194	115	359	2,213
PAR	4	4	4	4	4	3	4	3	5	35
HDCP	5	1	9	15	7	11	13	17	3	

HOLE	10	11	12	13	14	15	16	17	18	IN	TOTAL
WHITE	377	129	448	148	391	346	148	332	379	2,698	5,436
RED	363	99	430	132	374	279	94	314	313	2,398	4,611
PAR	4	3	5	3	4	4	3	4	4	34	69
HDCP	6	16	4	18	2	10	14	12	8		

RATES: Weekdays: 6–9 a.m.: $12 for 18, $7 for 9. 9 a.m.–2 p.m.: $16 for 18, $9 for 9. 2–4 p.m.: $12 for 18, $7 after 4 p.m. Weekends: $19 for 18, $10 for 9. $7 twilight. Carts: $20 for 18, $12 for 9.
FACILITIES: Putting green, golf lessons, pro shop, restaurant, bar, banquet facilities, locker rooms, club rental, golf equipment sold, tee time recommended on weekends and holidays.

ST. ANDREWS GOLF AND COUNTRY CLUB
3 NORTH 441 ROUTE 59
WEST CHICAGO, IL 60185
(708)231-3100

St. Andrews: 18-Hole Course, 6,403 Yards, Par 71, CDGA rating 70.3

Lakewood: 18-Hole Course, 6,425 Yards, Par 72, CDGA rating 70.1

LOCATION: IL Route 59, just north of the intersection of North Avenue and Route 59

SEASON: Open all year

GOLF PROFESSIONAL: Ron Skubisz

COURSE OWNER: Joe Jemsek

GREENS SUPERINTENDENT: John Lapp

St. Andrews has two 18-hole courses that are average in length but have some very long par-3 and par-4 holes. St. Andrews was built in 1928, and Lakewood opened in 1930. Both courses were originally designed by Edward B. Dearie, Jr., and remodeled in 1968 by Joe Lee. The current owner, Joe Jemsek, purchased the club in 1938. The courses are built on rolling hills with tree-lined fairways which vary from tight to open. Depending on which tees are used, the course can challenge the better player but is playable for the mid- to high handicapper. Shot placement on the large greens is a premium.

ST. ANDREWS SCORECARD:

HOLE	1	2	3	4	5	6	7	8	9	OUT
YARDS	328	431	158	377	289	398	182	467	397	3,027
PAR	4	4	3	4	4	4	3	5	4	35
HDCP	12	2	18	10	14	8	16	6	4	

HOLE	10	11	12	13	14	15	16	17	18	IN	TOTAL
YARDS	491	436	212	371	501	164	422	405	374	3,376	6,403
PAR	5	4	3	4	5	3	4	4	4	36	71
HDCP	7	1	15	13	5	17	3	9	11		

LAKEWOOD SCORECARD:

HOLE	1	2	3	4	5	6	7	8	9	OUT
YARDS	336	191	390	366	416	180	337	403	478	3,097
PAR	4	3	4	4	4	3	4	4	5	35
HDCP	12	16	8	10	2	18	14	4	6	

HOLE	10	11	12	13	14	15	16	17	18	IN	TOTAL
YARDS	462	197	316	311	191	502	443	526	380	3,328	6,425
PAR	5	3	4	4	3	5	4	5	4	37	72
HDCP	7	15	13	11	17	5	1	3	9		

RATES: Weekdays: $23, $12.50 after 3:30 p.m., $8.25 after 6:15 p.m. Weekends: $100 per foursome before 2:30 p.m., $19 per golfer after 2:30 p.m., $12.50 after 4 p.m., $8.25 after 6:15 p.m. Carts: $23, $16 after 3:30 p.m.

FACILITIES: Putting green, driving range, golf lessons, pro shop, restaurant, snack shop, bar, banquet facilities, locker rooms, club rental, golf equipment sold, tee time recommended, permanent tee time available.

SALT CREEK GOLF CLUB
18 WEST 700 THORNDALE AVENUE
WOOD DALE, IL 60191
(708)773-0184

Red: 9-Hole Course, 1,703 Yards, Par 28, CDGA rating N/A
White: 9-Hole Course, 3,807 Yards, Par 31, CDGA rating N/A
LOCATION: 2½ miles east of Route 53 on Thorndale Avenue
SEASON: March 1 through December 1
GOLF PROFESSIONAL: Tony Perry
COURSE OWNER: Wood Dale Park District
GREENS SUPERINTENDENT: Gary Hearn

On the last Friday of the month from April through October, Salt Creek holds what they call Nite-Lite Golf Tournaments on their 2 executive 9-hole courses. About 35 years ago, Salt Creek was built by a group of friends who toiled on weekends and after work to complete the course. The Wood Dale Park District purchased it in 1987 from Fred Lukins and since then has enlarged the tees and added sand traps. The course is flat with narrow, tree-lined fairways and 2 water hazards. The course record is 56, held jointly by club pro Tony Perry and Jack Skorberg.

RED COURSE SCORECARD:

HOLE	1	2	3	4	5	6	7	8	9	TOTAL
YARDS	268	170	195	161	157	243	148	223	138	1,703
PAR	4	3	3	3	3	3	3	3	3	28
HDCP	5	11	10	13	14	6	16	7	17	

WHITE COURSE SCORECARD:

HOLE	1	2	3	4	5	6	7	8	9	TOTAL
YARDS	204	268	153	387	124	279	169	203	317	2,104
PAR	3	4	3	4	3	4	3	3	4	31
HDCP	8	4	15	1	18	3	12	9	2	

RATES: Weekdays: $7, $6.50 replays. Seniors 9 a.m.–3 p.m.: $6, $5.50 replays. Juniors 9 a.m.–3 p.m.: $6, $5.50 replays. Weekends: $7.50, $7 replays. Resident rates available.
FACILITIES: Driving range, golf lessons, pro shop, restaurant, snack shop, bar, banquet facilities, club rental, golf equipment sold, fivesomes allowed, tee time recommended.

SEVEN BRIDGES GOLF CLUB
ONE MULLIGAN DRIVE
WOODRIDGE, IL 60517
(708)964-7777
FOR RESERVATIONS PHONE 964-GOLF

18-Hole Course, 7,118 Yards, Par 72, CDGA rating 74.1
LOCATION: Northwest of 75th Street and Old Route 53
SEASON: April through November
GOLF PROFESSIONAL: Roger Warren
COURSE OWNER: Village of Woodridge
GREENS SUPERINTENDENT: Don Ferreri

Situated on the majestic grounds of a historic country club and forest preserve, Seven Bridges was built under the direction of one of golf's foremost architects, Dick Nugent. Rolling hills, 100-year-old oak trees, water, water, and more water characterize this remarkable modern-day golf course. On the front 9 you'll encounter sand, water, and plenty of mature trees. The greens are heavily contoured and guarded on all sides by huge bunkers. On the back 9 it might be a good idea to bring a kayak, because you'll spend most of your time in the water. On numbers 10 through 16, you'll battle creeks, ponds, and lakes from tee to green. The greens are large, fast, and have two or three tiers. The service is first-rate at Seven Bridges and gives this public course a comfortable, private-club atmosphere.

SCORECARD:

HOLE	1	2	3	4	5	6	7	8	9	OUT
GOLD	531	378	188	392	403	183	469	449	579	3,572
GREEN	515	357	168	351	368	162	446	428	554	3,349
WHITE	492	325	154	333	336	150	424	402	524	3,140
RED	402	292	123	284	311	125	359	345	452	2,693
PAR	5	4	3	4	4	3	4	4	5	36
HDCP	5	13	17	9	11	15	1	7	3	

HOLE	10	11	12	13	14	15	16	17	18	IN	TOTAL
GOLD	517	412	554	210	427	165	441	373	447	3,546	7,118
GREEN	501	390	529	174	402	156	425	352	418	3,347	6,696
WHITE	473	370	503	161	379	133	404	341	389	3,153	6,293
RED	391	303	423	114	317	82	338	291	325	2,584	5,277
PAR	5	4	5	3	4	3	4	4	4	36	72
HDCP	6	8	2	18	10	14	4	16	12		

RATES: Weekdays: $58 per player, includes electric cart. Weekends: $58 per player, includes electric cart. Carts: mandatory at all times.

FACILITIES: Putting green, golf lessons, pro shop, restaurant, bar, banquet facilities, locker rooms, club rental, golf equipment sold, cart required, tee time required. There is a dress code of collared shirts, Bermuda-length shorts, and no cutoffs.

SPRINGBROOK GOLF COURSE
2240 83RD STREET
NAPERVILLE, IL 60565
(708)420-4215

18-Hole Course, 6,459 Yards, Par 72, CDGA rating 69.5
LOCATION: 20 miles west of the Loop
SEASON: April through November
GOLF PROFESSIONAL: Ed Provow
COURSE OWNER: Naperville Park District
GREENS SUPERINTENDENT: Jeff Smith

Owned and operated by the Naperville Park District, Springbrook was created by the golf design firm Packard Inc. and opened in 1973. Built on gently rolling land, Springbrook is a gradually maturing course in excellent condition. There are 9 water hazards—5 play over and 4 play laterally—and 21 sand traps protect the greens, which are smooth, fast, and require careful reading to conquer. The average player will enjoy playing here, and the scratch player will be challenged to shoot par from the championship tees.

SCORECARD:

HOLE	1	2	3	4	5	6	7	8	9	OUT
CHAMP.	370	513	431	194	556	349	191	385	421	3,410
REG.	348	498	412	173	514	323	165	363	391	3,187
WOMEN	316	450	379	138	484	283	134	334	361	2,879
PAR	4	5	4	3	5	4	3	4	4	36
HDCP	13	3	7	15	1	11	17	9	5	

HOLE	10	11	12	13	14	15	16	17	18	IN	TOTAL
CHAMP.	378	498	413	153	442	561	426	207	408	3,486	6,896
REG.	359	477	345	139	425	539	405	194	389	3,272	6,459
WOMEN	325	436	311	108	408	492	368	167	356	2,971	5,850
PAR	4	5	4	3	4	5	4	3	4	36	72
HDCP	12	6	14	18	2	4	10	16	8		

RATES: Weekdays: $18 for 18; $13 twilight; $13 for 9; seniors, $14; juniors, $10. Weekends: $25 for 18, $14 twilight. Carts: $18 for 18, $12 for 9.

FACILITIES: Putting green, driving range, golf lessons, pro shop, snack shop, bar, club rental, golf equipment sold, tee time recommended, permanent tee time available for residents only.

TAMARACK GOLF CLUB
24032 ROYAL WORLINGTON DRIVE
NAPERVILLE, IL 60564
(708)904-4000

18-Hole Course, 6,955 Yards, Par 70, CDGA rating 74.2

LOCATION: 8 miles south of I-88 on Route 59, just south of 103rd Street

SEASON: April through November

GOLF PROFESSIONAL: Joe Sterr

GREENS SUPERINTENDENT: Peter Mirkes III

David Gill designed this par-70 course featuring 5 sets of tees to challenge golfers of all skill levels. The fairways are well defined by sand and water, and the greens are large and heavily contoured. Owing to the 16 acres of water, virtually every hole requires good shot-making ability. If you have enough skill to avoid the water, you may find yourself in one of the 76 sand bunkers which dot the fairways and surround the greens. Tamarack is in excellent condition, especially for a course that's only 4 years old. The course record of 66 was set by Ken Metzger in 1989.

SCORECARD:

HOLE	1	2	3	4	5	6	7	8	9	OUT
BLACK	389	471	173	423	566	239	430	393	435	3,519
BLUE	350	443	129	377	541	180	386	364	396	3,166
WHITE	328	427	115	359	533	163	368	346	377	3,016
GOLD	300	378	100	307	477	145	335	307	342	2,691
RED	278	361	82	289	447	125	321	291	323	2,517
PAR	4	4	3	4	5	3	4	4	4	35
HDCP	13	1	17	9	3	15	11	7	5	

HOLE	10	11	12	13	14	15	16	17	18	IN	TOTAL
BLACK	565	204	613	429	197	388	456	196	388	3,436	6,955
BLUE	520	189	572	388	167	361	427	173	368	3,165	6,331
WHITE	501	165	558	371	153	342	408	161	348	3,007	6,023
GOLD	440	156	484	326	138	304	362	149	313	2,672	5,363
RED	421	140	461	309	121	286	342	127	292	2,499	5,016
PAR	5	3	5	4	3	4	4	3	4	35	70
HDCP	8	12	2	16	18	10	4	6	14		

RATES: Weekdays: $43. Senior citizens: Monday through Thursday, $25. Weekends: $48. Carts: included.

FACILITIES: Putting green, driving range, golf lessons, pro shop, restaurant, snack shop, bar, banquet facilities, locker rooms, club rental, golf equipment sold, tee time required. There is a dress code requiring no cutoffs or tank tops.

TIMBER TRAILS COUNTRY CLUB
11350 PLAINFIELD ROAD
LAGRANGE, IL 60525
(708)246-0275

18-Hole Course, 6,197 Yards, Par 71, CDGA rating 68.9
LOCATION: ½ mile west of Wolf Road and Plainfield Road
SEASON: April 1 through November 30
GOLF PROFESSIONAL: Tom Byrd
COURSE OWNER: Roger A. Anderson
GREENS SUPERINTENDENT: Don Hoffman

Timber Trails is very aptly named. More than 1,600 trees line the fairways and border the greens, making accuracy a must on this short 6,197-yard layout. The landscape was designed by golf course architect Robert Bruce Harris in 1931. It has changed ownership only once, in 1964, since its construction. Straight shooting and the ability to hit high and low will be rewarded. The greens vary in size depending on the length of the hole and are protected by traps and trees. A large creek borders numbers 6 and 7, and a pond figures into play on the par-3 11th hole. Shorter hitters can enjoy a big advantage at Timber Trails if they can keep the ball straight.

SCORECARD:

HOLE	1	2	3	4	5	6	7	8	9	OUT
WHITE	388	455	327	150	322	492	503	157	376	3,170
RED	365	414	294	135	303	450	457	139	365	2,922
PAR	4	4	4	3	4	5	5	3	4	36
HDCP	7	3	13	17	11	5	1	15	9	

HOLE	10	11	12	13	14	15	16	17	18	IN	TOTAL
WHITE	409	186	303	355	400	405	168	326	475	3,027	6,197
RED	358	135	283	339	359	377	158	306	408	2,723	5,645
PAR	4	3	4	4	4	4	3	4	5	35	71
HDCP	2	8	6	14	12	4	18	16	10		

RATES: Weekdays: $23, $14 after 3 p.m. Weekends: $28, $21 after 2 p.m., $14 after 4 p.m. Carts: single rider, $14; double riders, $23.
FACILITIES: Putting green, golf lessons, pro shop, snack shop, locker rooms, club rental, golf equipment sold, tee time required. The course has a dress code of collared shirts and shorts 2 inches from the knees. Shorts and shirts can both be rented.

VALLEY GREEN GOLF COURSE
314 KINGSWOOD DRIVE
NORTH AURORA, IL 60542
(708)897-3000

18-Hole Course, 3,831 Yards, Par 60, CDGA rating N/A
LOCATION: ½ mile north of the East-West tollway, 35 miles west of the Loop
SEASON: Open all year
COURSE OWNERS: Mike Douglas and Phil Talbot
GREENS SUPERINTENDENT: Steve Adams

Very popular with seniors and beginners, Valley Green is a short, 18-hole executive golf course open year-round. There are not many trees, and over the years many of the sand traps have been changed to grass bunkers. The course is basically flat and wide open with water hazards on 4 of the 18 holes. In 1989, Bill Jarhcow established the course record with 54.

SCORECARD:

HOLE	1	2	3	4	5	6	7	8	9	OUT
MEN	160	347	265	251	215	155	177	110	333	2,013
WOMEN	160	347	265	251	215	155	130	110	333	1,966
PAR	3	4	4	4	3	3	3	3	4	31
HDCP	13	6	16	18	1	9	2	15	11	

HOLE	10	11	12	13	14	15	16	17	18	IN	TOTAL
MEN	140	205	160	205	180	253	185	170	320	1,818	3,831
WOMEN	140	130	160	205	180	253	185	138	320	1,711	3,677
PAR	3	3	3	3	3	4	3	3	4	29	60
HDCP	14	3	10	4	7	17	5	8	12		

RATES: Weekdays: $11 for 18; $7 for 9 and for twilight; senior citizens, $5.50. Weekends: $14 for 18; $9 for 9 and for twilight.
FACILITIES: Putting green, driving range, golf lessons, pro shop, snack shop, club rental, golf equipment sold, fivesomes allowed.

VILLAGE GREENS OF WOODRIDGE GOLF COURSE
1575 WEST 75TH STREET
WOODRIDGE, IL 60517
(708)985-3610

18-Hole Course, 6,650 Yards, Par 72, CDGA rating 70.3
LOCATION: 25 miles west of Chicago
SEASON: Mid-March through mid-December
GOLF PROFESSIONAL: Mark Arentsen
COURSE OWNER: Village of Woodridge
GREENS SUPERINTENDENT: Bob Rigney

Formerly Maplecrest Lake Country Club, this course was purchased and renamed by the Village of Woodridge in 1973. Since being built in 1959, new trees have been planted and 3 lakes have been created as part of a long-range construction improvement program. For the most part, fairways are wide with some tree lines, and the terrain varies from flat to rolling hills. The greens and fairways are well trapped, and although there is not a lot of water on the course, it affects the player's strategy. The course is challenging—the slope rating is 118 from the championship tees—but suited to all players regardless of handicap.

SCORECARD:

HOLE	1	2	3	4	5	6	7	8	9	OUT
BLUE	378	483	443	168	438	503	219	382	359	3,373
WHITE	362	466	426	148	409	488	200	365	342	3,206
RED	346	449	409	129	392	473	180	348	325	3,051
PAR	4	5	4	3	4	5	3	4	4	36
HDCP	9	11	1	17	3	7	5	13	15	

HOLE	10	11	12	13	14	15	16	17	18	IN	TOTAL
BLUE	382	523	358	128	411	400	366	173	536	3,277	6,650
WHITE	367	471	341	117	398	381	347	163	499	3,084	6,290
RED	352	422	324	107	331	362	328	151	419	2,796	5,847
PAR	4	5	4	3	4	4	4	3	5	36	72
HDCP	14	6	16	18	2	4	12	10	8		

RATES: Weekdays: $22 for 18, $14.25 after 3 p.m., $12 for 9, $6.50 after 6 p.m. Weekends: $24 for 18, $17 after 3 p.m., $13 for 9 after 3 p.m., $7.50 after 6 p.m. Carts: $22 for 18, $14.50 for 9.

FACILITIES: Putting green, driving range, golf lessons, pro shop, restaurant, snack shop, bar, banquet facilities, locker rooms, club rental, golf equipment sold, tee time required on weekends, tee time recommended, permanent tee time available.

VILLAGE LINKS OF GLEN ELLYN
485 WINCHELL WAY
GLEN ELLYN, IL 60137
(708)469-8180

18-Hole Course, 6,933 Yards, Par 71, CDGA rating 73.5
9-Hole Course, 3,353 Yards, Par 36, CDGA rating 36.0
LOCATION: Park Boulevard ½ mile south of Roosevelt Road (IL 38)
SEASON: April through November
GOLF PROFESSIONAL: Ed Posh
DIRECTOR OF GOLF: Matt McCormick
COURSE OWNER: Village of Glen Ellyn
GREENS SUPERINTENDENT: Tim Kelly

Designed by David Gill and opened in 1967, Village Links consists of 27 holes of very challenging golf. This 18-hole course is one of the toughest courses in the Midwest, with the 12th-highest rating among private and public courses in the CDGA. Rolling terrain, narrow fairways, and an abundance of trees characterize this demanding layout. Ninety-six traps dot the fairways, protecting the greens, and 20 lakes come into play on 14 of the 18 holes. The course is designed and groomed for the serious, confident golfer. The extensive practice facilities include nearly an acre of putting greens, a practice sand trap, and an all-turf driving range.

SCORECARD:

HOLE	1	2	3	4	5	6	7	8	9	OUT
BLUE	370	515	205	470	355	528	391	170	365	3,369
WHITE	342	487	177	445	317	490	353	150	331	3,092
RED	314	457	149	412	290	435	310	130	293	2,790
PAR	4	5	3	4	4	5	4	3	4	36
HDCP	13	5	15	1	9	3	7	17	11	

HOLE	10	11	12	13	14	15	16	17	18	IN	TOTAL
BLUE	430	154	443	470	430	552	443	232	410	3,564	6,933
WHITE	396	116	405	455	403	525	410	182	377	3,269	6,361
RED	345	100	360	427	377	497	380	152	325	2,963	5,753
PAR	4	3	4	4	4	5	4	3	4	35	71
HDCP	14	18	12	2	10	4	6	16	8		

SCORECARD:

HOLE	1	2	3	4	5	6	7	8	9	TOTAL
BLUE	339	520	397	172	430	417	509	197	372	3,353
WHITE	318	495	373	147	403	387	483	172	348	3,126
RED	298	410	343	117	377	362	454	142	318	2,821
PAR	4	5	4	3	4	4	5	3	4	36
HDCP	8	2	4	9	1	3	5	7	6	

RATES: Weekdays: $30 for 18, $10 for 9. $5 after 6:30 p.m. every day on 9-hole course. Weekends: $32 for 18, $12 for 9. Carts: $22 for 18, $12 for 9.

FACILITIES: 4 putting greens, driving range, golf lessons, pro shop, restaurant, snack shop, banquet facilities, locker rooms, club rental, golf equipment sold, tee time required, permanent tee time available.

WEDGEWOOD GOLF COURSE
ROUTE 59 AND CATON FARM ROAD
JOLIET, IL 60435
(815)741-7270

18-Hole Course, 6,836 Yards, Par 72, CDGA rating 70.5

LOCATION: 2 miles west of Route 55 and 5 miles north of Route 80

SEASON: March through December

GOLF PROFESSIONAL: Ted Brodeur

COURSE OWNER: Joliet Park District

GREENS SUPERINTENDENT: Ken Shepherd

Wedgewood is a 6,836-yard, par-72 course that will allow you to use every club in your bag. The terrain is flat and the fairways are wide open for the most part, allowing you to use your driver liberally. The large greens are well bunkered and fairly easy to putt. The course has a large practice fairway and practice chipping area so you can warm up while waiting to tee off.

SCORECARD:

HOLE	1	2	3	4	5	6	7	8	9	OUT
BLUE	391	563	402	209	354	496	436	164	367	3,382
WHITE	378	545	386	172	340	486	422	146	350	3,225
RED	360	423	355	155	323	433	377	130	296	2,852
PAR	4	5	4	3	4	5	4	3	4	36
HDCP	7	3	1	13	15	9	5	17	11	

HOLE	10	11	12	13	14	15	16	17	18	IN	TOTAL
BLUE	388	510	441	230	368	532	424	159	402	3,454	6,836
WHITE	372	491	425	213	348	518	408	133	386	3,294	6,519
RED	350	467	384	183	290	420	360	117	369	2,940	5,792
PAR	4	5	4	3	4	5	4	3	4	36	72
HDCP	16	12	4	2	8	10	6	18	14		

RATES: Weekdays: resident, $9 for 18, $7.50 for 9; nonresident, $16 for 18, $11 for 9. Weekends: resident, $11 for 18, $9 for 9; nonresident: $19 for 18, $13 for 9. Carts: $16 for 18, $9 for 9.

FACILITIES: Putting green, driving range, golf lessons, pro shop, restaurant, snack shop, club rental, golf equipment sold, tee time required on weekends only.

WESTGATE VALLEY COUNTRY CLUB
1300 SOUTH RIDGELAND AVENUE
PALOS HEIGHTS, IL 60463
(708)385-1810

West: 18-Hole Course, 6,399 Yards, Par 71, CDGA rating 67.3
East: 18-Hole Course, 5,436 Yards, Par 67, CDGA rating N/A
LOCATION: 17 miles southwest of the Loop
SEASON: Open all year
GOLF PROFESSIONAL: Ken Buss
COURSE OWNERS: Tom Walsh Family Corporation
GREENS SUPERINTENDENT: Ron Austin

Westgate offers 36 holes of golf for the middle to high handicapper. The West Course is longer and more challenging than the East Course and features a good selection of trees with wide-open fairways. There are no sand traps to catch your shots and very little water to worry about on either course. The large greens make putting a little tricky, but there are plenty of birdie opportunities available here. Tee times are strongly recommended at this very busy public course.

WEST COURSE SCORECARD:

HOLE	1	2	3	4	5	6	7	8	9	OUT
YARDS	565	350	170	330	280	330	212	505	415	3,157
PAR	5	4	3	4	4	4	3	5	4	36
HDCP	1	13	11	9	17	15	3	7	5	

HOLE	10	11	12	13	14	15	16	17	18	IN	TOTAL
YARDS	425	422	410	140	435	325	205	355	525	3,242	6,399
PAR	4	4	4	3	4	4	3	4	5	35	71
HDCP	2	8	12	16	4	18	6	14	10		

EAST COURSE SCORECARD:

HOLE	1	2	3	4	5	6	7	8	9	OUT
YARDS	370	145	285	353	160	420	378	372	135	2,618
PAR	4	3	4	4	3	4	4	4	3	33
HDCP	8	16	12	10	14	2	6	4	18	

HOLE	10	11	12	13	14	15	16	17	18	IN	TOTAL
YARDS	380	300	155	395	350	335	138	355	410	2,818	5,436
PAR	4	4	3	4	4	4	3	4	4	34	67
HDCP	3	13	15	5	9	11	17	7	1		

RATES: Weekdays: West: $19 for 18, $10 after 3 p.m. East: $19 for 18, $9.50 for 9. Weekends: West: $22 for 18, $11 after 3 p.m. East: $22 for 18, $11 for 9. Carts: $21 for 18, $11 for 9.

FACILITIES: Putting green, indoor driving range, golf lessons, pro shop, restaurant, snack shop, bar, locker rooms, club rental, golf equipment sold, tee time recommended, permanent tee time available.

WILLOW RUN COUNTRY CLUB
187TH STREET, 1 1/2 MILES WEST OF WOLF ROAD
MOKENA, IL 60448
(815)485-2119

9-Hole Course, 2,950 Yards, Par 35, CDGA rating N/A
LOCATION: 40 miles southwest of the Loop
SEASON: April through November
GOLF PROFESSIONAL: Jack Kory
COURSE OWNERS: Neal Skvorc and Mike Smith
GREENS SUPERINTENDENT: Sonny Bain

Willow Run is a sporty, 9-hole daily fee course designed and maintained for the average golfer. Numbers 2 and 9 are the only water holes, and the course is lightly bunkered, but the numerous mature trees provide plenty of hazards. The greens are small, about 5,000 square feet, and the watered fairways are wide. Rough is kept light to keep play moving. The course was built in 1960 and purchased by the current owners in 1968 from the Langland family. Roger Sutton set the course record of 29 in 1972.

SCORECARD:

HOLE	1	2	3	4	5	6	7	8	9	TOTAL
MEN	420	140	305	190	410	300	340	325	520	2,950
WOMEN	420	140	305	190	410	300	340	325	420	2,850
PAR	4	3	4	3	4	4	4	4	5	35
HDCP	4	7	8	3	2	9	6	5	1	

RATES: Weekdays: $19.50 for 18, $11 for 9. Monday through Saturday: $10.50 after 3 p.m. Monday through Friday: seniors, $13 for 18, $8 for 9; juniors $15 for 18, $9 for 9. Weekends: $22 for 18, $12.50 for 9. Carts: $22 for 18, $12 for 9.

FACILITIES: Putting green, golf lessons, pro shop, restaurant, snack shop, bar, banquet facilities, locker rooms, club rental, golf equipment sold, tee time required weekends and holidays.

WOODBINE GOLF COURSE
14240 WEST 151ST STREET
LOCKPORT, IL 60441
(708)301-1252

18-Hole Course, 6,020 Yards, Par 70, CDGA rating 67.5
LOCATION: Between Cedar and Parker Roads
SEASON: March until November
COURSE OWNERS: Jim and Pat Ludwig, Sharon and Ted Mochel
GREENS SUPERINTENDENT: Ted Mochel

Woodbine was built in 1987 and is in very good condition for a newer course. The quality of the bent grass on the fairways and greens reflects meticulous care on the part of the greens superintendent. Although it was designed for the average golfer, the layout requires accuracy with its narrow fairways, well-trapped greens, and 5 lateral water hazards.

SCORECARD:

HOLE	1	2	3	4	5	6	7	8	9	OUT
REG.	505	283	374	156	420	392	409	157	381	3,077
WOMEN	482	263	339	138	399	370	390	134	360	2,875
PAR	5	4	4	3	4	4	4	3	4	35
HDCP	3	11	5	17	1	13	7	15	9	

HOLE	10	11	12	13	14	15	16	17	18	IN	TOTAL
REG.	378	370	141	512	139	501	162	340	400	2,943	6,020
WOMEN	357	350	102	493	127	472	140	318	384	2,743	5,618
PAR	4	4	3	5	3	5	3	4	4	35	70
HDCP	10	8	12	2	16	4	18	14	6		

RATES: Weekdays: $18 for 18; $13 for 9; $11 after 3 p.m.; seniors, $14 for 18, $9 for 9. Weekends: $22 for 18, $13 after 3 p.m. Carts: $10.50 per person, $13 for two riders.
FACILITIES: Putting green, pro shop, restaurant, snack shop, bar, banquet facilities, club rental, golf equipment sold, tee time recommended, permanent tee time available.

WOODRUFF GOLF COURSE
GOUGAR ROAD
JOLIET, IL 60433
(815)741-7272

18-Hole Course, 5,563 Yards, Par 68, CDGA rating 64.6
LOCATION: Between Route 6 and Route 30 on Gougar Road
SEASON: March 15 through December 1
COURSE OWNER: Joliet Park District
GREENS SUPERINTENDENT: Mike Conroy

Although the course is short, not too many people break 70 here. Streams wind through the course, creating hazards on 12 holes, and the thick stands of large trees and narrow fairways demand a straight-shooting game. Woodruff has been a public course since it opened in the mid-1920s and hosts several local tournaments.

SCORECARD:

HOLE	1	2	3	4	5	6	7	8	9	OUT
MEN	309	201	379	267	165	309	394	366	355	2,745
WOMEN	295	190	365	255	84	275	321	344	343	2,472
PAR	4	3	4	4	3	4	4	4	4	34
HDCP	11	15	4	14	17	13	2	6	8	

HOLE	10	11	12	13	14	15	16	17	18	IN	TOTAL
MEN	323	390	316	380	178	349	179	367	336	2,818	5,563
WOMEN	310	378	225	361	118	330	156	349	297	2,524	4,996
PAR	4	4	4	4	3	4	3	4	4	34	68
HDCP	10	1	12	5	18	9	16	3	7		

RATES: Weekdays: $16 for 18, $11 for 9. Weekends: $19 for 18, $13 for 9. Resident rates available. Carts: $16 for 18, $9 for 9.
FACILITIES: Putting green, golf lessons, pro shop, snack shop, club rental, golf equipment sold.

ZIGFIELD TROY GOLF COURSE
1535 75TH STREET
WOODRIDGE, IL 60517
(708)985-GOLF

9-Hole Course, 1,064 Yards, Par 27, CDGA rating N/A

LOCATION: ½ mile west of 75th and Lemont

SEASON: April through November

GOLF PROFESSIONALS: Dennis and Tim Troy

COURSE OWNER: The Troy Family

GREENS SUPERINTENDENT: Dennis Troy

Zigfield Troy is a family-owned golf range and par-3 executive course. The fairways are watered and wide open, and the greens are fast with challenging undulations. There are 9 bunkers factoring into play and 1 water hazard. A pond is a consideration on 2 of the 9 holes. The well-groomed greens are considered some of the best in the area.

SCORECARD:

HOLE	1	2	3	4	5	6	7	8	9	TOTAL
LONG	110	132	136	117	126	111	109	140	83	1,064
SHORT	71	101	126	106	79	106	103	130	72	894
PAR	3	3	3	3	3	3	3	3	3	27

RATES: Weekdays: $9 for 18, $5 for 9. Weekends: $10 for 18, $6 for 9. Carts: pull carts only, $1.

FACILITIES: Putting green, driving range, golf lessons, pro shop, golf equipment sold. Shirts are required.

Northwest

APPLE ORCHARD GOLF COURSE
696 STEARNS ROAD
BARTLETT, IL 60103
(708)837-6568

9-Hole Course, 1,360 Yards, Par 27, CDGA rating N/A
LOCATION: 30 miles west of the Loop
SEASON: April 1 through October 31
COURSE OWNER: Bartlett Park District

Apple Orchard is a short, par-3, 9-hole course with rolling terrain and open fairways. The greens are relatively small, and the many trees may present some difficulty. With just a few well-placed sand traps and 1 water hazard, the course is great for beginners or for polishing your short game.

SCORECARD:

HOLE	1	2	3	4	5	6	7	8	9	TOTAL
YARDS	160	135	195	100	170	205	140	125	130	1,360
PAR	3	3	3	3	3	3	3	3	3	27
HDCP	5	8	2	7	3	1	4	9	6	

RATES: Weekdays: residents, $4.50 and $4 for replays; nonresidents, $5 and $4.50 for replays. Weekends: residents, $5.50 and $5 for replays; nonresidents, $6 and $5.50 for replays.
FACILITIES: Putting green, golf lessons, banquet facilities, club rental.

ARBORETUM GOLF CLUB
401 HALF DAY ROAD
BUFFALO GROVE, IL 60089
(708)913-1112

18-Hole Course, 6,477 Yards, Par 72, CDGA rating 71.1

LOCATION: South side of Half Day Road, one light east of Buffalo Grove Road

SEASON: April through November

DIRECTOR OF GOLF: Carmen A. Molinaro

COURSE OWNER: Village of Buffalo Grove

GREENS SUPERINTENDENT: Richard Reed

Arboretum is a new course, designed by Dick Nugent and built in 1989. All tees, greens, and fairways are bent grass, and there are many mature trees despite the fact that it's a young course. The fairways are narrow, and water factors into play on 15 holes. The large greens are fast and surrounded by bunkers, making accuracy a must with approach shots. Arboretum is in excellent condition and while it is not extremely long, the trees, hills, and water make for an extremely challenging game. The course record of 69 was set in July of 1991 by Carmen Molinaro.

SCORECARD:

HOLE	1	2	3	4	5	6	7	8	9	OUT
CHAMP	404	506	418	353	207	391	159	387	526	3,351
BLUE	373	489	400	330	183	369	141	365	506	3,156
WHITE	344	473	385	310	163	342	128	347	481	2,973
RED	294	394	301	267	139	315	117	303	436	2,566
PAR	4	5	4	4	3	4	3	4	5	36
HDCP	7	5	1	15	11	13	17	9	3	

HOLE	10	11	12	13	14	15	16	17	18	IN	TOTAL
CHAMP	314	526	371	343	127	357	538	161	389	3,126	6,477
BLUE	297	505	354	318	113	335	518	151	366	2,957	6,113
WHITE	276	493	332	294	102	312	498	130	350	2,787	5,760
RED	255	432	293	269	90	278	437	112	307	2,473	5,039
PAR	4	5	4	4	3	4	5	3	4	36	72
HDCP	14	4	8	12	16	10	2	18	6		

RATES: Weekdays: $30 for 18, $17 for 9. Weekends: $33 for 18, $20 after 4 p.m., $13 after 6 p.m. Carts: $20 for 18, $10 for 9.

FACILITIES: Putting green, golf lessons, pro shop, snack shop, bar, club rental, golf equipment sold, tee time required. There is a dress code of no tank tops and no rubber spikes.

ARLINGTON LAKES GOLF COURSE
1211 SOUTH NEW WILKE ROAD
ARLINGTON HEIGHTS, IL 60005
(708)577-3030

18-Hole Course, 4,976 Yards, Par 68, CDGA rating 65.5
LOCATION: 3 blocks north of Algonquin Road
SEASON: April through November
GOLF PROFESSIONAL: Jim Hoch
COURSE OWNER: Arlington Heights Park District
GREENS SUPERINTENDENT: Butch Peuvion

Designed by David Gill and built in 1979, Arlington Lakes is short but challenging. The course lives up to its name with 14 lakes which come into play on most of the holes. The watered fairways are narrow, and the terrain is rolling. Greens are small and well guarded with 105 sand traps on the course. Mostly small trees flank the fairways, and an additional 200 to 500 are planted each year. Arlington Lakes is a short course rewarding accuracy and shot selection.

SCORECARD:

HOLE	1	2	3	4	5	6	7	8	9	OUT
YARDS	373	168	353	264	129	252	331	157	434	2,461
PAR	4	3	4	4	3	4	4	3	5	34
HDCP	3	13	5	9	17	11	7	15	1	

HOLE	10	11	12	13	14	15	16	17	18	IN	TOTAL
YARDS	328	463	110	360	140	389	311	105	309	2,515	4,976
PAR	4	5	3	4	3	4	4	3	4	34	68
HDCP	8	2	16	6	14	4	12	18	10		

RATES: Weekdays: $17 for 18, $9.50 for 9 and after 4 p.m. Weekends: $19 for 18, $10.50 for 9 and after noon. Resident rates available. Carts: weekdays, $16 for 18, $10 for 9; weekends, $18 for 18, $11 for 9.
FACILITIES: Putting green, driving range, golf lessons, pro shop, restaurant, snack shop, bar, banquet facilities, locker rooms, club rental, golf equipment sold, tee time recommended.

BONNIE DUNDEE GOLF AND COUNTRY CLUB
ILLINOIS HIGHWAYS 25 AND 68
DUNDEE, IL 60118
(708)426-5511

18-Hole Course, 6,176 Yards, Par 70, CDGA rating 68.1
LOCATION: 37 miles northwest of the Loop
SEASON: Open all year
GOLF PROFESSIONAL: Jim Ervin
GREENS SUPERINTENDENT: Nick DiVito

Set on 110 acres, Bonnie Dundee is Scottish in design with gently rolling terrain, numerous grass bunkers, and nearly 50 sand traps. The course sits on a gravel base which holds moisture and provides excellent drainage. Only the tees and greens are watered, and the fairways are as lush as you will find in the Chicago area. The greens are medium sized but quite narrow on this well-manicured course featuring maples along with a variety of other trees and bushes. Designed by Charles Dudley Wagstaff in 1925, Bonnie Dundee has plenty of character.

SCORECARD:

HOLE	1	2	3	4	5	6	7	8	9	OUT
YARDS	433	430	388	383	334	359	403	137	192	3,059
PAR	5	4	4	4	4	4	4	3	3	35
HDCP	14	7	13	3	2	4	10	18	9	

HOLE	10	11	12	13	14	15	16	17	18	IN	TOTAL
YARDS	414	154	364	548	410	284	385	176	382	3,117	6,176
PAR	4	3	4	5	4	4	4	3	4	35	70
HDCP	16	1	6	12	17	11	5	15	8		

RATES: Weekdays: $14, $10 after 3 p.m. Weekends: $20, $12 after 3 p.m. Carts: $16.
FACILITIES: Putting green, pro shop, restaurant, snack shop, bar, banquet facilities, locker rooms, club rental, golf equipment sold, tee time required on weekends, tee time recommended.

BRISTOL OAKS COUNTRY CLUB
16801 75TH STREET
BRISTOL, WI 53104
(414)857-2302

18-Hole Course, 6,187 Yards, Par 72, CDGA rating 69.2
LOCATION: 2½ miles west of I-94 on Highway 50
SEASON: Open all year
COURSE OWNERS: Roger Chisholm and William Seawall
GREENS SUPERINTENDENT: Len Eibl

Located just west of Interstate 94 in Bristol, Wisconsin, Bristol Oaks features hilly terrain and open fairways. At 6,187 yards starting from the back tees, the course is not overwhelming, but even the best players will find it difficult to two-putt the large, fast greens. Water comes into play on numbers 8, 11, and 17, and sand is not much of a factor.

SCORECARD:

HOLE	1	2	3	4	5	6	7	8	9	OUT
BLUE	389	488	290	481	338	175	324	151	366	3,002
WHITE	378	471	280	467	323	155	315	135	356	2,880
RED	367	453	270	453	308	134	306	119	346	2,756
PAR	4	5	4	5	4	3	4	3	4	36
HDCP	5	3	13	1	9	15	11	17	7	

HOLE	10	11	12	13	14	15	16	17	18	IN	TOTAL
BLUE	406	287	484	184	403	160	490	365	406	3,185	6,187
WHITE	390	274	467	173	392	142	471	351	393	3,053	5,933
RED	374	261	449	163	381	102	452	337	380	2,899	5,655
PAR	4	4	5	3	4	3	5	4	4	36	72
HDCP	4	16	10	14	2	18	8	12	6		

RATES: Weekdays: $12. Weekends: $17. Carts: $19.
FACILITIES: Putting green, driving range, golf lessons, pro shop, restaurant, snack shop, bar, banquet facilities, locker rooms, club rental, golf equipment sold, cart required on weekends, tee time required. There is a dress code that shirts are required.

BUFFALO GROVE GOLF CLUB
48 RAUPP BOULEVARD
BUFFALO GROVE, IL 60089
(708)459-5520

18-Hole Course, 6,892 Yards, Par 72, CDGA rating 71.5
LOCATION: Lake Cook Road, 2 stoplights west of Route 83
SEASON: All year
DIRECTOR OF GOLF: Carmen Molinaro
COURSE OWNER: Village of Buffalo Grove
GREENS SUPERINTENDENT: Richard Reed

Built in 1965 and designed by golf course architects Ken Killian and Dick Nugent, Buffalo Grove is fairly long with more bunkers and water than you'll find on most public courses. The watered fairways are wide open and lined with mature trees. Several doglegs lead to small, fast, flat greens guarded by deep greenside bunkers. Buffalo Grove is a well-kept course which is challenging for players of all skill levels.

SCORECARD:

HOLE	1	2	3	4	5	6	7	8	9	OUT
BLUE	410	490	400	220	540	363	390	170	420	3,403
WHITE	390	480	380	200	520	350	370	150	400	3,240
RED	370	470	360	180	500	337	350	105	380	3,052
PAR	4	5	4	3	5	4	4	3	4	36
HDCP	7	3	9	13	1	15	11	17	5	

HOLE	10	11	12	13	14	15	16	17	18	IN	TOTAL
BLUE	450	395	520	380	180	409	555	155	445	3,489	6,892
WHITE	430	375	500	360	160	385	485	135	425	3,255	6,495
RED	400	305	460	340	140	331	465	105	405	2,951	6,003
PAR	4	4	5	4	3	4	5	3	4	36	72
HDCP	6	12	2	14	16	10	4	18	8		

RATES: Weekdays: $17 for 18, $10 for 9; senior citizens, $11 for 18, $7.25 for 9. Weekends: $21 for 18, $17.75 after 1 p.m., $10 after 3 p.m. Carts: $20 for 18, $10 for 9.
FACILITIES: Putting green, driving range, golf lessons, pro shop, restaurant, snack shop, bar, banquet facilities, locker rooms, club rental, golf equipment sold, tee time recommended, permanent tee time available. The dress code is shirts are required and no rubber shoes.

CARY COUNTRY CLUB
2400 GROVE LANE
CARY, IL 60013
(708)639-3161

18-Hole Course, 6,135 Yards, Par 72, CDGA rating 67.9
LOCATION: 35 miles northwest of the Loop
SEASON: April through November
GOLF PROFESSIONAL: Robert Keith
COURSE OWNER: Group ownership
GREENS SUPERINTENDENT: Tom Vieweg

Cary Country Club is a well-maintained, quality golf course with hilly terrain and large trees. The watered fairways are wide open, leaving some room for error off the tees. There are 50 bunkers placed strategically on the fairways and around the small greens. In addition to the traps are 4 water hazards that can also create some problems. Skill rather than strength is needed to score well at Cary.

SCORECARD:

HOLE	1	2	3	4	5	6	7	8	9	OUT
WHITE	489	325	293	167	382	138	486	297	539	3,116
RED	449	287	273	158	369	125	403	237	493	2,794
PAR	5	4	4	3	4	3	5	4	5	37
HDCP	7	11	14	16	5	18	1	9	3	

HOLE	10	11	12	13	14	15	16	17	18	IN	TOTAL
WHITE	378	316	167	486	179	296	411	403	383	3,019	6,135
RED	365	308	155	452	132	286	389	395	372	2,854	5,648
PAR	4	4	3	5	3	4	4	4	4	35	72
HDCP	8	13	17	2	15	12	6	4	10		

RATES: Weekdays: $17 for 18, $11 for 9 and after 4 p.m. Weekends: $20 for 18, $14 after 4 p.m.; $15 for 9 holes after 5 p.m. includes cart. Carts: $20 for 18, $11 for 9.

FACILITIES: Putting green, golf lessons, pro shop, restaurant, snack shop, bar, banquet facilities, locker rooms, club rental, golf equipment sold, tee time required on weekends, permanent tee time available.

CHAPEL HILL COUNTRY CLUB
2500 NORTH CHAPEL HILL ROAD
MCHENRY, IL 60050
(815)385-3337

18-Hole Course, 6,021 Yards, Par 70, CDGA rating 67.4
LOCATION: 4 miles west of Route 12 on Route 120
SEASON: April through November
COURSE OWNER: K. C. Bae
GREENS SUPERINTENDENT: Ron Doruff

Chapel Hill is a semiprivate club offering dining room, lounge, and banquet facilities with a seating capacity of 250. The course was built in 1950 and was purchased by the current owners in June of 1990. The terrain is flat for the most part and the fairways are wide, but the course is tightly laid out. There are 16 sand bunkers protecting the small, bent-grass greens, and two ponds come into play on numbers 9 and 14. Although the course is short, measuring just over 6,000 yards from the back tees, number 17 is a 605-yard par 5 that even the longest hitters will find very difficult to birdie. Overall, the course is well suited to the high handicapper.

SCORECARD:

HOLE	1	2	3	4	5	6	7	8	9	OUT
BLUE	410	431	435	225	302	365	351	191	480	3,190
WHITE	386	416	413	202	277	349	344	161	470	3,018
RED	376	402	401	190	255	339	333	145	403	2,844
PAR	4	4	4	3	4	4	4	3	5	35
HDCP	3	5	2	12	16	10	7	17	4	

HOLE	10	11	12	13	14	15	16	17	18	IN	TOTAL
BLUE	135	345	353	235	340	280	322	605	216	2,831	6,021
WHITE	135	335	343	228	327	268	317	562	193	2,708	5,726
RED	116	324	336	220	307	253	299	482	178	2,515	5,359
PAR	3	4	4	4	4	4	4	5	3	35	70
HDCP	18	8	6	15	9	13	11	1	14		

RATES: Weekdays: $16 for 18, $10 for 9, $9 after 4 p.m. Weekends: $20 for 18, $13 for 9 after 3 p.m., $11 after 4 p.m. Carts: $20 for 18; $14 for 9; pull carts, $2.50. Carts required until 1 p.m. on weekends.

FACILITIES: Putting green, driving range, pro shop, restaurant, snack shop, bar, banquet facilities, locker rooms, club rental, golf equipment sold, cart required on weekends, tee time recommended. The dress code is shirts are required and no tank tops.

CHEVY CHASE GOLF COURSE
1000 NORTH MILWAUKEE AVENUE
WHEELING, IL 60090
(708)537-0082

18-Hole Course, 6,721 Yards, Par 72, CDGA rating 71.4
LOCATION: 45 miles northwest of the Loop
SEASON: April through November
GOLF PROFESSIONAL: Vernon Verstraete
COURSE OWNERS: Wheeling Park District
GREENS SUPERINTENDENT: Tom McDonald

Chevy Chase was purchased by the Wheeling Park District in 1977 from private ownership. The course was in extremely poor condition but has undergone remarkable improvement in the last decade. In addition to an extensive tree-planting program, all the tees and sand traps have been rebuilt. There are 56 sand traps on the course, but not all the greens are bunkered. The terrain is flat, and the fairways are wide open. Water will be your main enemy with 14 of 18 holes affected. It is necessary to hit your drive over water off of 9 tees. From the blue tees the course is long—6,721 yards—testing the skills of any golfer.

SCORECARD:

HOLE	1	2	3	4	5	6	7	8	9	OUT
BLUE	374	514	448	521	454	140	360	418	131	3,360
GOLD	360	478	411	495	434	124	332	363	121	3,118
WHITE	346	415	341	425	364	99	311	310	71	2,682
PAR	4	5	4	5	4	3	4	4	3	36
HDCP	11	7	1	5	3	17	13	9	18	

HOLE	10	11	12	13	14	15	16	17	18	IN	TOTAL
BLUE	409	363	447	201	349	490	152	371	579	3,361	6,721
GOLD	362	343	384	187	319	475	143	343	563	3,119	6,237
WHITE	314	280	291	121	275	425	128	329	489	2,652	5,334
PAR	4	4	4	3	5	4	3	4	5	36	72
HDCP	8	14	6	12	15	4	16	10	2		

RATES: Weekdays: $17 for 18, $12 for 9, $10 after 6 p.m. Seniors: $13 for 18, $10 for 9. Juniors: $11 for 18, $7 for 9. Weekends: $22 for 18, $16 2–4 p.m., $10 after 4 p.m. Carts: weekdays, $17 for 18, $12 for 9; weekends, $22.

FACILITIES: Putting green, driving range, golf lessons, pro shop, restaurant, snack shop, bar, banquet facilities, locker rooms, club rental, golf equipment sold, permanent tee time available.

CRYSTAL WOODS GOLF CLUB
5915 SOUTH ROUTE 47
WOODSTOCK, IL 60098
(815)338-3111

18-Hole Course, 6,150 Yards, Par 72, CDGA rating 68.2
LOCATION: 10 minutes north of Route 47 from I-90 (Northwest tollway)
SEASON: St. Patrick's Day through Thanksgiving
GOLF PROFESSIONAL: John Craig
COURSE OWNERS: Richard and Mary Ann Craig
GREENS SUPERINTENDENT: Ignacio Carreno

Crystal Woods is a beautifully maintained course, providing a stiff challenge to the average golfer. This course features medium- sized greens, mature trees, and gently rolling hills with fairly tight fairways and well-placed bunkers. Three additional fairway bunkers are being added to the right side of the 5th hole to make it more difficult. Water comes into play on 6 holes with hazards jealously guarding the 8th and 12th greens, making them the most difficult holes on the course. Crystal Woods was the site of the 1984 Illinois Qualifier, and John Craig and Steve Thompson share the course record of 64.

SCORECARD:

HOLE	1	2	3	4	5	6	7	8	9	OUT
BLUE	360	405	345	173	560	365	164	487	313	3,172
WHITE	352	389	331	170	553	356	156	475	302	3,084
RED	338	295	283	139	419	314	146	421	282	2,637
PAR	4	4	4	3	5	4	3	5	4	36
HDCP	9	3	7	15	1	13	17	5	11	

HOLE	10	11	12	13	14	15	16	17	18	IN	TOTAL
BLUE	508	201	405	120	355	510	187	350	505	3,141	6,313
WHITE	500	194	398	115	349	501	179	335	495	3,066	6,150
RED	452	180	386	95	338	440	166	329	465	2,851	5,488
PAR	5	3	4	3	4	5	3	4	5	36	72
HDCP	6	10	2	18	14	4	12	16	8		

RATES: Weekdays: $17 for 18, $10 for 9. Weekends: $33 before 2 p.m. includes cart, $17 after 2 p.m., $12 after 5 p.m. Carts: $22 for 18, $12 for 9.
FACILITIES: Putting green, driving range, golf lessons, pro shop, restaurant, snack shop, banquet facilities, golf equipment sold, cart required on weekends, tee time required on weekends, tee time recommended, permanent tee time available.

FOX LAKE COUNTRY CLUB
7220 STATE PARK ROAD
FOX LAKE, IL 60020
(708)587-6411

18-Hole Course, 6,347 Yards, Par 72, CDGA rating 71.2
LOCATION: ½ mile north of Route 12 in Lake County
SEASON: April through November
GOLF MANAGER: Joseph A. Petrungaro
COURSE OWNER: Charles E. Petrungaro
GREENS SUPERINTENDENT: Ray Kearney

Fox Lake is among the finest public golf courses in the Chicago area. The course is fully irrigated with finely groomed fairways and greens. The gently rolling terrain and undulating elevated greens require precision iron play to parlay your shots into birdies and pars. The 5 water hazards and 57 sand traps will test your skill and try your patience on this heavily wooded layout. The course is somewhat difficult but very fair if you make intelligent shots.

SCORECARD:

HOLE	1	2	3	4	5	6	7	8	9	OUT
BLUE	323	372	102	424	443	465	494	179	335	3,137
WHITE	316	362	94	415	432	451	483	165	331	3,049
YELLOW	309	352	86	406	421	437	472	150	327	2,960
PAR	4	4	3	4	4	5	5	3	4	36
HDCP	14	16	18	8	4	6	2	10	12	

HOLE	10	11	12	13	14	15	16	17	18	IN	TOTAL
BLUE	340	195	499	314	179	371	302	484	526	3,210	6,347
WHITE	326	175	492	306	167	356	293	472	520	3,107	6,156
YELLOW	306	160	485	287	150	246	284	460	514	2,892	5,852
PAR	4	3	5	4	3	4	4	4	5	36	72
HDCP	15	7	5	9	17	11	13	1	3		

RATES: Weekdays: 18 holes with cart, $35. Weekends: 18 holes with cart, $45. Carts: mandatory at all times.
FACILITIES: Putting green, driving range, pro shop, restaurant, snack shop, bar, banquet facilities, locker rooms, club rental, golf equipment sold, cart required, tee time required. The dress code is shirts must be worn at all times and no tank tops.

FOX RUN GOLF LINKS
333 PLUM GROVE ROAD
ELK GROVE VILLAGE, IL 60007
(708)980-GOLF

18-Hole Course, 6,350 Yards, Par 70, CDGA rating N/A
LOCATION: 25 miles northwest of the Loop
SEASON: Late March through November
CLUBHOUSE MANAGER: Ed Hauser
COURSE OWNER: Elk Grove Park District
GREENS SUPERINTENDENT: Greg Thalmann

Built in 1984, Fox Run was designed by William Newcomb and provides a true test of accuracy and strategy. The terrain is flat, and the watered fairways on the front 9 are quite narrow. A major concern on the back 9 is water, which comes into play on 7 of those holes. There are 67 sand traps protecting the large greens. Good club selection is essential in order to score well on this sporty course. Although relatively new, Fox Run has matured quickly with numerous trees and shrubs planted each year since its inception. Upon completion, cart paths will be continuous from holes 1 through 18.

SCORECARD:

HOLE	1	2	3	4	5	6	7	8	9	OUT
BLUE	380	403	219	509	403	167	372	339	361	3,153
WHITE	362	390	203	498	389	152	354	320	345	3,013
RED	312	321	168	453	345	134	303	296	319	2,651
PAR	4	4	3	5	4	3	4	4	35	4
HDCP	9	7	5	1	3	17	11	15	13	

HOLE	10	11	12	13	14	15	16	17	18	IN	TOTAL
BLUE	404	483	392	390	415	194	343	180	396	3,197	6,350
WHITE	390	472	378	374	385	167	328	164	379	3,027	6,040
RED	361	426	335	318	354	131	288	144	316	2,673	5,324
PAR	4	5	4	4	4	3	4	3	4	35	70
HDCP	2	4	8	12	10	14	18	16	6		

RATES: Weekdays: $18 for 18, $11 after 4 p.m. and for 9. Weekends: $22 for 18, $13 after 4 p.m. Resident rates available. Carts: $20 for 18, $11 for 9.
FACILITIES: Putting green, driving range, golf lessons, pro shop, snack shop, bar, banquet facilities, club rental, golf equipment sold, tee time recommended.

GOLF CLUB OF ILLINOIS
1575 EDGEWOOD ROAD
ALGONQUIN, IL 60102
(708)658-4400

18-Hole Course, 6,558 Yards, Par 71, CDGA rating 71.1

LOCATION: 1 mile west of IL 31 at intersection of Edgewood Road and Hanson Road

SEASON: March through November

GOLF PROFESSIONAL: Winston Howe III

GREENS SUPERINTENDENT: Greg Johnson

Golf Digest rated the Golf Club of Illinois one of the 10 best new public courses in the country. Designed by Dick Nugent and Bruce Borland, the course was opened in 1987 and has matured quickly. It is of Scottish design demanding both length and accuracy. The fairways are bent grass oval targets surrounded by bluegrass rough. Rugged terrain flanks the rough, water comes into play on 4 holes, and 105 bunkers cover the greens, which range from small to medium in size. The Golf Club of Illinois hosted the 1988 Illinois Open and boasts the longest par 5 in North America: hole 15, a brutal 678 yards from the championship tee. Reminiscent of Scotland, this course tests character and ability.

SCORECARD:

HOLE	1	2	3	4	5	6	7	8	9	OUT
GOLD	448	535	451	175	467	196	375	390	431	3,468
WHITE	422	508	425	142	441	184	364	372	411	3,269
RED	350	460	332	119	388	145	349	352	350	2,845
PAR	4	5	4	3	4	3	4	4	4	35
HDCP	7	1	5	17	3	15	13	11	9	

HOLE	10	11	12	13	14	15	16	17	18	IN	TOTAL
GOLD	537	351	203	366	340	678	393	228	447	3,543	7,011
WHITE	507	326	171	339	323	647	373	183	420	3,289	6,558
RED	449	306	140	312	308	612	343	75	369	2,914	5,759
PAR	5	4	3	4	4	5	4	3	4	36	71
HDCP	4	12	18	10	14	2	8	16	6		

RATES: Monday through Thursday: $28 for 18 and $12 cart mandatory until noon; $16 for 9, $7 for 9-hole cart. Friday, Saturday, Sunday: $38 for 18 and $12 cart mandatory until 2 p.m.; $22 for 9, $7 for 9-hole cart.

FACILITIES: Putting green, driving range, golf lessons, pro shop, restaurant, snack shop, bar, banquet facilities, locker rooms, club rental, golf equipment sold, cart required, tee time required, permanent tee time available.

123

HILLDALE COUNTRY CLUB
1655 ARDWICK DRIVE
HOFFMAN ESTATES, IL 60195
(708)310-1100

18-Hole Course, 5,862 Yards, Par 71, CDGA rating 68.1
LOCATION: 30 miles northwest of the Loop
SEASON: April through November
GOLF PROFESSIONAL: John Wedell
COURSE OWNER: Chicago Kosaido Corporation
GREENS SUPERINTENDENT: Al Bevers

Accuracy is essential on this course since water comes into play on nearly every hole. In addition to the 80 to 90 sand traps which protect the greens, Hilldale has tight fairways lined with trees, condominiums, and townhouses. The bent-grass greens are elevated and average in size with gently rolling to hilly terrain. Architect Robert Trent Jones, who also designed Pebble Beach, intended for Hilldale to provide a challenging round of golf; it does that and more.

SCORECARD:

HOLE	1	2	3	4	5	6	7	8	9	OUT
BLUE	367	546	381	140	329	352	400	169	389	3,073
WHITE	331	535	355	122	309	336	384	139	359	2,870
RED	290	497	315	95	290	295	335	109	329	2,555
PAR	4	5	4	3	4	4	4	3	4	35
HDCP	16	2	8	18	12	10	4	14	6	

HOLE	10	11	12	13	14	15	16	17	18	IN	TOTAL
BLUE	390	602	379	187	514	311	188	421	346	3,338	6,411
WHITE	368	558	356	167	460	297	173	410	321	3,110	5,980
RED	312	420	333	147	406	283	145	405	297	2,748	5,303
PAR	4	5	4	3	5	4	3	4	4	36	71
HDCP	3	1	11	9	5	15	17	13	7		

RATES: Weekdays: $22 for 18, $12 for 9. Weekends: $29 for 18; $19 after 4 p.m.; $15 for 9. Carts: $22 for 18 (required every day before 3 p.m.), $12 for 9.
FACILITIES: Putting green, driving range, golf lessons, pro shop, restaurant, snack shop, bar, banquet facilities, locker rooms, club rental, golf equipment sold, cart required daily until 3 p.m., tee time required, permanent tee time available.

KEMPER LAKES
OLD MCHENRY ROAD
HAWTHORN WOODS, IL 60047
(708)540-3450

18-Hole Course, 6,680 Yards, Par 72, CDGA rating 73.8
LOCATION: In Lake County north of Route 22 and west of Route 83
SEASON: April through November
GOLF PROFESSIONAL: Emil Esposito
COURSE OWNER: Kemper Group
GREENS SUPERINTENDENT: Doug Quiram

Site of the 1989 PGA Championship, Kemper Lakes is a 10-year-old public course designed by Ken Killian and Dick Nugent. The course is long—7,217 yards from the championship tees—and tough, with beautifully manicured greens and fairways. Three lakes create water hazards on 8 holes, and the fairways are fairly open off the tees. *Golf Digest* rates Kemper Lakes number 99 among the nation's top 100 courses.

SCORECARD:

HOLE	1	2	3	4	5	6	7	8	9	OUT
GOLD	406	380	173	508	442	180	557	421	448	3,515
BLUE	378	357	141	496	423	166	513	392	428	3,294
WHITE	361	334	112	475	406	153	500	367	411	3,119
RED	346	329	106	435	349	150	450	279	395	2,839
PAR	4	4	3	5	4	3	5	4	4	36
HDCP	11	13	17	9	5	15	1	7	3	

HOLE	10	11	12	13	14	15	16	17	18	IN	TOTAL
GOLD	453	534	393	219	420	578	469	203	433	3,702	7,217
BLUE	416	502	369	183	377	557	426	172	384	3,386	6,680
WHITE	380	454	364	165	345	542	405	142	349	3,146	6,265
RED	337	442	308	131	326	492	363	82	318	2,799	5,638
PAR	4	5	4	3	4	5	4	3	4	36	72
HDCP	10	4	16	18	14	6	2	12	8		

RATES: Every day: $90 includes cart.
FACILITIES: Putting green, driving range, golf lessons, pro shop, restaurant, snack shop, bar, banquet facilities, locker rooms, club rental, golf equipment sold, cart required, foursomes only, tee time required, permanent tee time available.

LAKE PARK GOLF COURSE
1175 HOWARD
DES PLAINES, IL 60018
(708)827-7930

18-Hole Course, 1,515 Yards, Par 54, CDGA rating N/A
LOCATION: 10 miles northwest of the Loop, 2 minutes from I-294
SEASON: April 1 through October 31
GOLF PROFESSIONAL: Gene Zuccarini
COURSE OWNER: Des Plaines Park District
GREENS SUPERINTENDENT: John Kiraly

Lake Park is a par-3 course that totals just over 1,500 yards. The terrain is flat, and the watered fairways are narrow. Water runs all along the back 9, and the greens are small. Many bunkers were added in 1980 making some holes more difficult. The course record is 48, shot by Gene Zuccarini in 1964. Lake Park is golf for all golfers: beginners can practice on a course that is more suited to their ability, and seasoned golfers will find it great for honing their short game.

SCORECARD:

HOLE	1	2	3	4	5	6	7	8	9	OUT
YARDS	110	77	55	106	80	61	84	92	95	760
PAR	3	3	3	3	3	3	3	3	3	27
HDCP	10	14	1	4	13	16	9	8	7	

HOLE	10	11	12	13	14	15	16	17	18	IN	TOTAL
YARDS	115	64	54	100	111	76	85	79	71	755	1,515
PAR	3	3	3	3	3	3	3	3	3	27	54
HDCP	12	18	11	5	17	2	15	6	3		

RATES: Weekdays: $5.50; seniors and juniors (8 a.m.–4 p.m.), $4. Weekends: $6.50.
FACILITIES: Putting green, golf lessons, pro shop, snack shop, club rental.

MARENGO RIDGE GOLF AND COUNTRY CLUB
9508 HARMONY HILL ROAD
MARENGO, IL 60152
(815)923-2332

9-Hole Course, 3,250 Yards, Par 36, CDGA rating 35.4
LOCATION: 35 miles northwest of O'Hare Airport
SEASON: March through December 15
GOLF PROFESSIONAL: Charles Nihan
COURSE OWNER: Bob Witek
GREENS SUPERINTENDENT: Ken Loeffel

Marengo Ridge was a 9-hole course that expanded to 18 holes in 1990. The original 9 was designed by William James Spear and built in 1964. It is a semiprivate course that has been under constant renovation including new tees and continuous tree planting. Rolling terrain and watered fairways—a combination of narrow and open outlined by 2-inch-high rough—offer panoramic views of the Fox Valley. The greens are average in size and well protected by many of the 45 sand traps on the course. Six lakes and 2 waterways add to the difficulty and character of Marengo, which will challenge all levels of golfers. A new clubhouse is scheduled to open in the spring of 1992, and fairway homesites are available on this lush, wooded course.

SCORECARD:

HOLE	1	2	3	4	5	6	7	8	9	OUT
CHAMP.	445	180	390	545	395	240	455	410	550	3,610
TOUR.	430	165	375	530	380	225	440	395	535	3,475
CLUB	410	150	360	490	350	200	390	380	520	3,250
FWRD.	390	130	340	470	330	180	370	360	500	3,070
PAR	4	3	4	5	4	3	4	4	5	36
HDCP	4	18	10	12	14	6	2	16	8	

HOLE	10	11	12	13	14	15	16	17	18	IN	TOTAL
CHAMP.	423	525	373	160	320	518	423	215	422	3,379	6,989
TOUR.	400	522	358	145	311	512	400	176	413	3,237	6,712
CLUB	369	505	325	120	292	475	368	159	381	2,994	6,244
FWRD.	352	447	302	118	257	443	340	137	356	2,752	5,822
PAR	4	5	4	3	4	5	4	3	4	36	72
HDCP	11	7	15	13	17	1	3	5	9		

RATES: Weekdays: $15.50 for 18; $8.50 for 9; seniors, $7 for 9. Weekends: $17.50 for 18, $9.50 for 9. Carts: $18 for 18, $10 for 9.

FACILITIES: Putting green, driving range, golf lessons, pro shop, restaurant, snack shop, bar, banquet facilities, locker rooms, club rental, golf equipment sold, tee time recommended, permanent tee time available.

OLD ORCHARD COUNTRY CLUB
700 WEST RAND ROAD
MT. PROSPECT, IL 60056
(708)255-2025

18-Hole Course, 6,022 Yards, Par 71, CDGA rating 69.5
LOCATION: 25 miles northwest of the Loop
SEASON: April through November
GOLF PROFESSIONAL: Marc Heidkamp
COURSE OWNER: Glenn Steinberg
GREENS SUPERINTENDENT: Jerry Arden

Old Orchard is a well-manicured, championship-quality course. The terrain is basically flat, and the watered fairways are tight. Although not extremely long, this heavily wooded course is quite challenging with water coming into play on 10 holes. The greens are small and fast, protected by 38 strategically placed sand traps. Old Orchard is in excellent condition and was designed to require accuracy and good club selection.

SCORECARD:

HOLE	1	2	3	4	5	6	7	8	9	OUT
BLUE	387	358	159	375	379	457	193	350	516	3,174
RED	375	353	142	331	371	439	183	339	495	3,028
WHITE	363	332	100	278	363	424	173	330	474	2,837
PAR	4	4	3	4	4	5	3	4	5	36
HDCP	5	13	17	11	3	9	15	7	1	

HOLE	10	11	12	13	14	15	16	17	18	IN	TOTAL
BLUE	282	211	323	444	139	487	319	230	413	2,848	6,022
RED	271	200	311	433	120	478	313	205	360	2,691	5,719
WHITE	260	189	299	422	99	469	307	167	348	2,560	5,397
PAR	4	3	4	5	3	5	4	3	4	35	71
HDCP	18	10	16	6	14	2	12	8	4		

RATES: Weekdays: $41 for 18 (includes cart which is mandatory), $16 for 9, $12 for cart. Weekends: $46 for 18 (includes cart which is mandatory), $20 for 9, $12 for cart.
FACILITIES: Putting green, driving range, golf lessons, pro shop, restaurant, snack shop, bar, banquet facilities, locker rooms, club rental, golf equipment sold, cart required, tee time recommended, permanent tee time available.

PALATINE HILLS GOLF COURSE
512 WEST NORTHWEST HIGHWAY
PALATINE, IL 60067
(708)359-4020

18-Hole Course, 6,520 Yards, Par 72, CDGA rating 70.6
LOCATION: 20 to 25 miles northwest of the Loop
SEASON: April until December
GOLF PROFESSIONAL: Len Fiocca
COURSE OWNER: Palatine Park District
GREENS SUPERINTENDENT: Brad Helms

Designed by Chicago architect Roger Packard, Palatine Hills opened in 1968. The course was built on hilly terrain and features a variety of mature trees and streams. Fairways vary from tight to wide open, and trap placement around the large greens makes it fairly easy to pitch and roll onto them. The 18-hole layout measures 6,800 yards from the back tees and has a slope rating of 118. Gary Hallberg set the course record with 66.

SCORECARD:

HOLE	1	2	3	4	5	6	7	8	9	OUT
BLUE	395	415	520	165	465	540	185	330	375	3,390
WHITE	380	400	505	150	440	525	170	320	360	3,250
RED	350	365	470	135	385	490	145	295	335	2,970
PAR	4	4	5	3	4	5	3	4	4	36
HDCP	7	5	13	17	1	11	9	15	3	

HOLE	10	11	12	13	14	15	16	17	18	IN	TOTAL
BLUE	405	365	555	240	410	505	400	145	385	3,410	6,800
WHITE	390	350	540	205	405	490	385	135	370	3,270	6,520
RED	370	310	510	175	380	450	340	115	355	3,005	5,975
PAR	4	4	5	3	4	5	4	3	4	36	72
HDCP	6	16	12	10	8	14	2	18	4		

RATES: Monday through Thursday: $19.50 for 18, $11 for 9 and after 4 p.m. Friday through Sunday: $22 for 18, $12 for 9 and after 4 p.m. Carts: $20 for 18, $11 for 9.
FACILITIES: Putting green, golf lessons, pro shop, snack shop, bar, locker rooms, club rental, golf equipment sold, tee time recommended, permanent tee time available.

PINECREST GOLF AND COUNTRY CLUB
11220 ALGONQUIN ROAD
HUNTLEY, IL 60142
(708)669-3111 OR (708)669-3113

18-Hole Course, 6,044 Yards, Par 72, CDGA rating 68.7
LOCATION: 50 miles northwest of the Loop
SEASON: March until November
GOLF PROFESSIONAL: Mike Yackle
COURSE OWNER: James Huseman Family
GREENS SUPERINTENDENT: Brian Comiskey

Pinecrest was designed by Edward G. "Ted" Lockie in 1972 and has never looked better. The course reflects meticulous care and ongoing change. Recent improvements include 2 rebuilt holes, some narrowed fairways, and new trees and bunkers. The course features rolling terrain, and the watered fairways are fairly open. In order to reach the large greens you'll need to shoot over water on 6 holes and avoid 60 sand traps. Pinecrest is always in excellent condition, and the white tees allow the average golfer to enjoy the game and have the opportunity to score well.

SCORECARD:

HOLE	1	2	3	4	5	6	7	8	9	OUT
BLUE	380	593	368	488	413	195	413	116	390	3,356
WHITE	340	517	336	472	393	175	383	101	363	3,080
RED	249	406	285	403	327	159	320	89	275	2,513
PAR	4	5	4	5	4	3	4	3	4	36
HDCP	7	5	11	13	3	15	1	17	9	

HOLE	10	11	12	13	14	15	16	17	18	IN	TOTAL
BLUE	403	203	340	183	302	407	550	359	533	3,280	6,636
WHITE	370	161	301	163	279	351	491	336	512	2,964	6,044
RED	301	106	228	147	262	332	402	318	452	2,548	5,061
PAR	4	3	4	3	4	4	5	4	5	36	72
HDCP	8	12	10	16	18	2	4	14	6		

RATES: Weekdays: $18 for 18, $9 for 9. Weekends: $35 for 18 (includes cart which is mandatory before 2 p.m.), $18 after 2 p.m., $12 for 9 after 2 p.m. only. Carts: $14 for 9, $8 single; $22 for 18, $14 single.
FACILITIES: Putting green, driving range, golf lessons, pro shop, restaurant, snack shop, bar, banquet facilities, locker rooms, club rental, golf equipment sold, tee time recommended, permanent tee time available.

PISTAKEE COUNTRY CLUB
815 WEST BAY ROAD
MCHENRY, IL 60050
(815)385-9854

9-Hole Course, 3,027 Yards, Par 36, CDGA rating 34.6
LOCATION: U.S. 12 to 134, west 2½ miles on 134
SEASON: When playable
GOLF PROFESSIONAL: Harry C. Nielsen
COURSE OWNER: Harry C. Nielsen
GREENS SUPERINTENDENT: Harry George Nielsen

Pistakee is a hilly, 9-hole course that is situated in a heavily wooded area with watered fairways and fairly wide openings to the greens. This 67-year-old course comprises medium-sized, well- maintained greens, 15 sand traps, and 1 water hazard. Harry C. Nielsen has owned Pistakee since 1971, and the course record is 30 (6 under par) shot by Pat Westin. Although it is not an easy course, Pistakee gives the average golfer an opportunity to score well.

SCORECARD:

HOLE	1	2	3	4	5	6	7	8	9	TOTAL
YARDS	490	370	420	140	420	190	255	290	452	3,027
PAR	5	4	4	3	4	3	4	4	5	36
HDCP	2	3	4	7	1	6	9	8	5	

RATES: Weekdays: $9. Weekends: $10. Carts: $10.
FACILITIES: Putting green, pro shop, restaurant, snack shop, bar, golf equipment sold, tee time recommended, permanent tee time available.

PLUM TREE NATIONAL GOLF COURSE
19511 LEMBCKE ROAD, ROUTE 14
HARVARD, IL 60033
(815)943-7474 OR 1-800-851-3578

18-Hole Course, 6,399 Yards, Par 72, CDGA rating 70.9

LOCATION: Northwest of Chicago

SEASON: April through October

GOLF PROFESSIONAL: George Jackson

COURSE OWNER: Plum Tree National Ltd.

GREENS SUPERINTENDENT: Edward Schaefer

Built in 1969 and designed by Joe Lee, Plum Tree National is a championship-caliber course. The architect also designed some of America's top courses, including the famous Trophy Club in Fort Worth, Texas. Plum Tree features rolling terrain with lush, wide-open fairways and large greens. More than 100 sand traps dot the fairways and surround the greens, making accuracy on tee and approach shots very important. The many trees and water hazards can also create some problems, especially on the 8th hole, which is described by the *Chicago Sun-Times* as one of the toughest in the Chicago area. Plum Tree has been used for United States Open qualifying rounds, and it has a slope rating of 128 from the blue tees.

SCORECARD:

HOLE	1	2	3	4	5	6	7	8	9	OUT
BLUE	419	365	523	173	390	508	151	368	398	3,295
WHITE	400	350	511	160	376	496	140	357	386	3,176
RED	378	326	492	139	361	450	123	338	366	2,973
PAR	4	4	5	3	4	5	3	4	4	36
HDCP	7	13	5	15	11	1	17	3	9	

HOLE	10	11	12	13	14	15	16	17	18	IN	TOTAL
BLUE	386	387	547	173	393	405	366	184	512	3,353	6,653
WHITE	372	373	532	158	372	391	352	173	500	3,223	6,399
RED	350	350	509	134	293	372	334	159	480	2,981	5,954
PAR	4	4	5	3	4	4	4	3	5	36	72
HDCP	12	10	2	18	6	8	14	16	4		

RATES: Weekdays: $20 for 18, $12 for 9 and after 4 p.m. Weekends: $40 for 18, $35 after 2 p.m. (rates include carts, required on weekends). Carts: weekdays, $24 for 18, $16 for 9.

FACILITIES: Putting green, driving range, golf lessons, pro shop, restaurant, snack shop, bar, banquet facilities, locker rooms, club rental, golf equipment sold, cart required on weekends, foursomes only, tee time recommended, permanent tee time available.

POPLAR CREEK COUNTRY CLUB
1400 ERIC DRIVE
HOFFMAN ESTATES, IL 60194
(708)884-0219

18-Hole Course, 6,074 Yards, Par 70, CDGA rating 69.6

LOCATION: South of Northwest tollway, ½ mile east of Higgins Road

SEASON: Mid-March through mid-November

GOLF PROFESSIONAL: Jim Karras

COURSE OWNER: Hoffman Estates Park District

GREENS SUPERINTENDENT: Luke Strojny

Poplar Creek was built in 1976 and opened as the Moon Lake Golf Course. It was purchased in 1984 by Poplar Creek Joint Venture and renamed Poplar Creek Country Club. The Hoffman Estates Park District purchased the club in 1990. When it was known as Moon Lake, it was a young course that needed improving. During the past few years over 2 million dollars have been spent on improvements, and the course is becoming well known for its fine conditions. It isn't very long, but you have to be a disciplined shot maker to score well. Water comes into play on 14 holes, and the course is known for its many well-positioned bunkers. Out-of-bounds limits affect play on 15 holes. A new 30,000-square-foot clubhouse will open in the spring of 1992.

SCORECARD:

HOLE	1	2	3	4	5	6	7	8	9	OUT
BLUE	486	201	346	379	367	332	406	187	387	3,091
WHITE	476	183	320	336	352	318	378	143	329	2,835
RED	466	154	296	253	337	304	360	117	324	2,611
PAR	5	3	4	4	4	4	4	3	4	35
HDCP	3	5	13	11	7	15	1	17	9	

HOLE	10	11	12	13	14	15	16	17	18	IN	TOTAL
BLUE	402	338	362	171	344	356	161	488	361	2,983	6,074
WHITE	387	313	342	163	328	340	147	473	348	2,841	5,676
RED	372	271	252	155	312	324	121	458	335	2,600	5,211
PAR	4	4	4	3	4	4	3	5	4	35	70
HDCP	2	8	12	16	10	4	18	14	6		

134

RATES: Weekdays: resident: $14 for 18, $9 for 9, $9 after 4 p.m.; juniors and seniors: $12 for 18, $7 for 9; nonresident: $18 for 18, $11 for 9, $10 after 4 p.m. Weekends: resident: $18 for 18, $10 for 9 after 3 p.m., $10 for 18 after 4 p.m.; nonresident: $22 for 18, $13 for 9 after 3 p.m., $12 for 18 after 4 p.m. Carts: $20 for 18, $12 for 9. Pull carts: $2.50 for 18, $1.50 for 9.

FACILITIES: Putting green, driving range, golf lessons, pro shop, restaurant, snack shop, bar, banquet facilities, locker rooms, club rental, golf equipment sold, cart required on weekends, tee time recommended, permanent tee time available.

RAMADA HOTEL O'HARE GOLF COURSE
6600 NORTH MANNHEIM
ROSEMONT, IL 60018
(708)827-5131

9-Hole Course, 707 Yards, Par 27, CDGA rating N/A
LOCATION: Corner of Mannheim and Higgins, next to I-90
SEASON: April until October
COURSE OWNER: Ramada
GREENS SUPERINTENDENT: Tony Zerante

Ramada O'Hare is a par-3, 9-hole course that covers just over 700 yards. The terrain is basically flat, and there are very few trees to worry about. The course is wide open although some fairway approaches were cut in 1987. The greens are small and fairly well bunkered with 1 water hazard coming into play on 3 holes. Ramada O'Hare is a fun course and well suited to working on your short game. It is the only lighted course in the area intended for night play—a great place to spend those hot summer evenings.

SCORECARD:

HOLE	1	2	3	4	5	6	7	8	9	TOTAL
REG.	65	70	110	85	90	50	72	85	80	707
PAR	3	3	3	3	3	3	3	3	3	27
HDCP	8	7	1	9	5	6	2	4	3	

RATES: Every day: $6, $4 replays.
FACILITIES: Putting green, pro shop, restaurant, bar, banquet facilities, club rental, fivesomes allowed.

RANDALL OAKS GOLF CLUB
37W361 BINNIE ROAD
DUNDEE, IL 60118
(708)428-5661

18-Hole Course, 6,146 Yards, Par 71, CDGA rating 67.7
LOCATION: 1½ miles north of I-90 on Randall Road
SEASON: March through November
GOLF PROFESSIONAL: Phil Simonsen
COURSE OWNER: Dundee Township Park District
GREENS SUPERINTENDENT: Mike Sprouse

This sporty 18-hole course features front and back 9s with very distinct characteristics. The front 9 is hilly with narrow fairways, while the back 9 is flat and wide open. The undulating greens are fast and average in size. This well-conditioned course is 6,146 yards long and is best suited for the middle to high handicapper.

SCORECARD:

HOLE	1	2	3	4	5	6	7	8	9	OUT
BLUE	367	469	355	168	331	451	380	155	357	3,033
WHITE	357	460	345	155	316	438	366	150	342	2,929
RED	343	448	331	137	280	393	336	138	291	2,697
PAR	4	5	4	3	4	5	4	3	4	36
HDCP	5	3	13	17	9	1	11	15	7	

HOLE	10	11	12	13	14	15	16	17	18	IN	TOTAL
BLUE	379	433	341	161	373	506	359	174	387	3,113	6,146
WHITE	367	421	332	147	355	491	349	158	372	2,992	5,921
RED	351	325	320	115	315	451	335	136	334	2,682	5,379
PAR	4	4	4	3	4	5	4	3	4	35	71
HDCP	8	4	10	18	14	2	12	16	6		

RATES: Weekdays: Resident: $13 for 18, $8 for 9; after 4 p.m., $7.50; juniors and seniors, $7.50. Nonresident: $17 for 18, $11 for 9; after 4 p.m., $10.50; juniors and seniors, $11.50. Weekends: Resident: $17.50 for 18; after 4 p.m., $8.50; juniors and seniors after 4 p.m., $8.00. Nonresident: $21 for 18; after 4 p.m., $11.50; juniors and seniors after 4 p.m., $11. Carts: $20 for 18, $11 for 9. Pull carts: $2.50 for 18, $1.50 for 9.

FACILITIES: Putting green, driving range, golf lessons, pro shop, restaurant, snack shop, bar, banquet facilities, locker rooms, club rental, golf equipment sold, tee time required, permanent tee time available.

ROB ROY GOLF COURSE
505 EAST CAMP McDONALD ROAD
PROSPECT HEIGHTS, IL 60070
(708)253-4544

9-Hole Course, 3,126 Yards, Par 36, CDGA rating 69.7

LOCATION: ¼ mile east of Route 83, ½ mile west of Wolf Road

SEASON: April through November 15

GOLF PROFESSIONAL: Pierre Wener

COURSE OWNER: River Trails Park District

GREENS SUPERINTENDENT: Thomas A. Snyders

Rob Roy is a 9-hole park district course with narrow fairways surrounded by houses. The water hazards consist of a creek on the 180-yard, par-3 3rd hole and ponds on numbers 5 and 8. The course was built in 1926 and was purchased by the River Trails Park District in 1989. Jim Hahn holds the course record of 30.

SCORECARD:

HOLE	1	2	3	4	5	6	7	8	9	TOTAL
MEN	374	377	180	339	531	376	137	315	497	3,126
WOMEN	332	342	122	231	430	271	105	254	392	2,479
PAR	4	4	3	4	5	4	3	4	5	36
HDCP	5	3	8	6	1	4	9	7	2	

RATES: Weekdays: $15 for 18, $8.50 for 9. Weekends: $17 for 18, $9.50 for 9. Carts: $20 for 18, $10 for 9.

FACILITIES: Putting green, driving range, golf lessons, pro shop, bar, locker rooms, club rental, golf equipment sold, tee time recommended. Shirts are required.

ROLLING KNOLLS COUNTRY CLUB
ROUTE 1, BOX 319
ELGIN, IL 60120
(708)888-2888

18-Hole Course, 4,127 Yards, Par 66, CDGA rating N/A

LOCATION: Between Golf (Hwy 58) and Irving Park (Hwy 19) on Rohrssen Road, 1 mile west of Route 59

SEASON: April through November

COURSE OWNER: Tim Schneider

GREENS SUPERINTENDENT: Tom Schneider

Rolling Knolls was built in 1963 as a 9-hole course and recently expanded to a full 18 holes which opened in September 1989. True to its name, the course is laid out on rolling hills in a heavily wooded area, and many of the new holes are well bunkered. The tree-lined fairways are narrow and the greens are small, with water coming into play on 9 holes. Rolling Knolls is very short, but the tight fairways require precision.

SCORECARD:

HOLE	1	2	3	4	5	6	7	8	9	OUT
YARDS	242	335	203	460	343	287	217	218	82	2,387
PAR	4	4	3	5	4	4	3	4	3	34

HOLE	10	11	12	13	14	15	16	17	18	IN	TOTAL
YARDS	233	128	109	232	275	249	95	168	251	1,740	4,127
PAR	4	3	3	4	4	4	3	3	4	32	66

RATES: Weekdays: $14 for 18, $8 for 9. Weekends: $18 for 18, $10 for 9. Carts: $18 for 18, $9 for 9.

FACILITIES: Golf lessons, pro shop, restaurant, snack shop, bar, banquet facilities, club rental, golf equipment sold, tee time recommended, permanent tee time available.

SCHAUMBURG GOLF CLUB
401 NORTH ROSELLE ROAD
SCHAUMBURG, IL 60193
(708)885-9000

Front 9: 3,045 Yards, Par 36, CDGA rating N/A
Back 9: 3,083 Yards, Par 36, CDGA rating N/A
LOCATION: On Roselle Road, 3 blocks south of Route 72
SEASON: March 1 through December 1
GOLF PROFESSIONAL: Pepi Irwin
COURSE OWNER: Schaumburg Park District
GREENS SUPERINTENDENT: Nick Hongisto

Originally opened in 1926 as Westmore Country Club and later changed to Golden Acres Country Club, the course was most recently purchased by the Schaumburg Park District and renamed Schaumburg Golf Club. Over the past 2 years, extensive renovations have been made to the course, and 9 of the 27 holes are currently being built. Eighteen holes are open during renovation of the third 9. A large clubhouse and banquet facility is also currently under construction and due to be completed in late 1992.

SCORECARD:

HOLE	1	2	3	4	5	6	7	8	9	OUT
YARDS	530	350	140	510	295	120	410	285	405	3,045
PAR	5	4	3	5	4	3	4	4	4	36

HOLE	10	11	12	13	14	15	16	17	18	IN	TOTAL
YARDS	366	475	387	335	133	378	511	153	345	3,083	6,128
PAR	4	5	4	4	3	4	5	3	4	36	72

RATES: Weekdays: $15 for 18, $9 for 9. Weekends: $19 for 18, $16 after 4 p.m. Carts: double riders, $20 for 18, $12 for 9; single rider, $14.
NOTE: 1992 season rates are not yet established.
FACILITIES: Putting green, golf lessons, pro shop, snack shop, bar, banquet facilities, locker rooms, club rental, golf equipment sold, tee time recommended, permanent tee time available.

SPARTAN MEADOWS GOLF COURSE
Spartan Drive
Elgin, IL 60123
(708)931-5950

18-Hole Course, 6,672 Yards, Par 72, CDGA rating 71.1
LOCATION: ¼ mile south of Route 20 at intersection of Spartan Drive
and McLean Boulevard
SEASON: April through November
GOLF PROFESSIONAL: Rick Bell
COURSE OWNER: City of Elgin
GREENS SUPERINTENDENT: Jack Hughes

Spartan Meadows is a challenging course for all players. Designed by Edward Lawrence Packard and built in 1971, this par-72 layout measures 6,672 yards from the championship tees. You'll find water on 8 holes. Five ponds, 1 creek, and 27 bunkers jealously guard the bent-grass greens. The course is not heavily contoured, the terrain is mostly flat, and the wide-open fairways offer generous landing areas for your tee shots. There are some trees, but not enough to adversely affect your score.

SCORECARD:

HOLE	1	2	3	4	5	6	7	8	9	OUT
BLUE	395	527	354	152	403	432	508	191	372	3,334
WHITE	387	518	342	143	390	420	500	182	359	3,241
RED	372	502	284	127	276	400	486	147	336	2,930
PAR	4	5	4	3	4	4	5	3	4	36
HDCP	12	6	10	18	4	2	8	16	14	

HOLE	10	11	12	13	14	15	16	17	18	IN	TOTAL
BLUE	381	522	161	345	562	358	181	431	397	3,338	6,672
WHITE	372	509	154	336	550	346	172	411	385	3,235	6,476
RED	356	469	130	320	535	326	156	389	365	3,046	5,976
PAR	4	5	3	4	5	4	3	4	4	36	72
HDCP	11	7	17	13	3	9	15	1	5		

RATES: Weekdays: $12.50 for 18, $7.50 for 9, $8 twilight. Junior and senior rates available. Weekends: $19 for 18, $12 twilight. Carts: $20 for 18, $10 for 9.
FACILITIES: Putting green, driving range, golf lessons, pro shop, snack shop, club rental, golf equipment sold, tee time recommended. Shirts required.

141

THUNDERBIRD COUNTRY CLUB
1010 EAST NORTHWEST HIGHWAY
BARRINGTON, IL 60010
(708)381-6500

18-Hole Course, 6,169 Yards, Par 71, CDGA rating 68.6
LOCATION: On Route 14 between Route 68 and Route 59
SEASON: Open all year
GOLF PROFESSIONAL: Steve Dau
COURSE OWNER: Trumak Corporation
GREENS SUPERINTENDENT: Dennis Wimmer

Thunderbird dates back to before World War I and was purchased by the current owners in 1963. The course is built on rolling hills, and mature trees line several fairways. The several short par 4s will yield some birdies, and the overall length—6,169 yards—is not too intimidating. Many of the small greens are elevated, and the relatively small number of greenside bunkers make it fairly easy to get up and down if you miss the green. Eight water hazards come into play on 7 holes making the course difficult enough to challenge good players.

SCORECARD:

HOLE	1	2	3	4	5	6	7	8	9	OUT
BLUE	366	427	300	169	313	505	327	152	450	3,009
WHITE	353	411	286	163	295	493	315	141	296	2,753
PAR	4	4	4	3	4	5	4	3	4	35
HDCP	11	4	16	10	14	6	12	18	2	

HOLE	10	11	12	13	14	15	16	17	18	IN	TOTAL
BLUE	386	490	337	131	376	526	365	162	387	3,160	6,169
WHITE	338	425	307	123	316	468	359	148	296	2,780	5,533
PAR	4	5	4	3	4	5	4	3	4	36	71
HDCP	8	1	15	17	9	3	7	13	5		

RATES: Weekdays: $18 for 18, $10 for 9; senior citizens, $15 for 18, $9 for 9. Weekends: $24 for 18; after 2 p.m., $18 for 18, $10 for 9. Carts: two riders, $22 for 18, $11 for 9; one rider, $16 for 18, $9 for 9.

FACILITIES: Putting green, driving range, golf lessons, pro shop, restaurant, snack shop, bar, banquet facilities, locker rooms, club rental, golf equipment sold, tee time recommended, permanent tee time available.

TWIN PONDS GOLF CENTER
4411 NORTHWEST HIGHWAY
CRYSTAL LAKE, IL 60014
(815)455-1110

9-Hole Course, 1,351 Yards, Par 28, CDGA rating N/A
LOCATION: At the intersection of Routes 14 and 31
SEASON: March through November
GOLF PROFESSIONAL: John Swenson
COURSE OWNER: Walter Smith

Twin Ponds is a 9-hole, par-3 course with hilly terrain and wide fairways. There are only a few trees scattered around the course, and 7 sand bunkers guard 5 of the greens. The 2 large water hazards come into play on numbers 1, 3, 4, and 5 and create most of the trouble you'll face here. This course is perfect for beginners or for those who want to work on their short game.

SCORECARD:

HOLE	1	2	3	4	5	6	7	8	9	TOTAL
MENS	160	104	170	135	120	136	260	165	101	1,351
LADIES	160	104	140	100	120	136	231	165	101	1,257
PAR	3	3	3	3	3	3	4	3	3	28
HDCP	1	9	3	4	7	6	5	2	8	

RATES: Weekdays: $6; replay, $4; senior citizens, $4.50. Weekends: $7; replay, $4; senior citizens, $5.50. Carts: $8.75; pull cart, $2.
FACILITIES: Putting green, driving range, golf lessons, pro shop, restaurant, snack shop, bar, club rental, golf equipment sold, tee time required on weekends.

VILLA OLIVIA COUNTRY CLUB
U.S. HIGHWAY 20 AND NAPERVILLE ROAD
BARTLETT, IL 60103
(708)289-5200

18-Hole Course, 6,042 Yards, Par 72, CDGA rating 69.5

LOCATION: South of Lake Street (Hwy 20) and west of Route 59

SEASON: April through November

COURSE OWNER: Corrado Family

GREENS SUPERINTENDENT: Ed Joerns

Villa Olivia is a well-maintained, fairly wooded course that totals just over 5,600 yards and consists of mostly rolling hills. The fairways and the openings to the averaged-sized greens are wide, leaving some room for error, but 40 sand traps are placed strategically in the fairways and around the greens. Water comes into play on 6 holes, making the course a fair test for the average golfer.

SCORECARD:

HOLE	1	2	3	4	5	6	7	8	9	OUT
WHITE	295	518	400	361	482	167	327	169	489	3,208
RED	283	509	374	337	453	159	317	153	403	2,988
PAR	4	5	4	4	5	3	4	3	5	37
HDCP	17	5	1	7	9	15	13	3	11	

HOLE	10	11	12	13	14	15	16	17	18	IN	TOTAL
WHITE	142	234	359	473	315	393	122	368	428	2,834	6,042
RED	131	221	345	458	309	340	100	309	418	2,631	5,619
PAR	3	4	4	5	4	4	3	4	4	35	72
HDCP	16	18	2	10	14	6	12	8	4		

RATES: Weekdays: $22 for 18, $14 after 3 p.m.; $12.50 for 9, $11 after 4:30 p.m. Weekends: $24 for 18, $12 after 4 p.m. Carts: $22 for 18, $13.50 for 9 and for twilight. Carts are mandatory on weekends.

FACILITIES: Putting green, pro shop, restaurant, snack shop, bar, banquet facilities, locker rooms, club rental, golf equipment sold, cart required on weekends, tee time recommended, permanent tee time available.

WALNUT GREENS
1150 NORTH WALNUT LANE
SCHAUMBURG, IL 60194
(708)490-7878

9-Hole Course, 1,180 Yards, Par 27, CDGA rating N/A
LOCATION: 25 miles northwest of the Loop
SEASON: April through November
GOLF MANAGER: Eileen Sloan
COURSE OWNER: Schaumburg Park District
GREENS SUPERINTENDENT: Cherie Sheldon
ASSISTANT: Cherie Sheldon

Walnut Greens is a fun and sporty 9-hole, par-3 course. It is short but somewhat demanding with water designed as the main obstacle. The terrain is flat, and there are just 6 sand traps on the course. The fairways are narrow, but the greens are of good size. It is a great place to work on your short game, and alternate tees on 3 holes allow beginners to avoid much of the water. This short course plays in less than 2 hours, making it perfect for a round of golf before or after work.

SCORECARD:

HOLE	1	2	3	4	5	6	7	8	9	TOTAL
REG.	150	110	130	125	145	90	145	100	185	1,180
ALT	130	110	80	100	145	90	145	100	185	1,085
PAR	3	3	3	3	3	3	3	3	3	27
HDCP	2	7	5	6	4	9	3	8	1	

RATES: Weekdays: $6 for 9; juniors and seniors, $5 for 9. Weekends: $8 for 9; juniors and seniors, $6 for 9. Resident and family rates available.

FACILITIES: Putting green, pro shop, snack shop, club rental.

WILMETTE GOLF COURSE
3900 FAIRWAY DRIVE
WILMETTE, IL 60091
(708)256-9777

18-Hole Course, 6,072 Yards, Par 70, CDGA rating 68.8
LOCATION: ½ mile west of Edens, north edge of Cook County
SEASON: April through October
COURSE OWNER: Wilmette Park District
GOLF PROFESSIONAL: Kermit L. Shettel
GREENS SUPERINTENDENT: Michael Matchen

Formerly owned by Northwestern University, Wilmette Golf Course was purchased by the Wilmette Park District in 1973. The course has undergone extensive renovation throughout the past 15 years, and the improvement is evident. Situated on flat terrain, the course features narrow fairways and medium to large greens. It is a sporty course with plenty of bunkers and 6 water hazards. Wilmette Golf Course is heavily orientated to serve Wilmette residents, with nonmember tee times only available on weekdays.

SCORECARD:

HOLE	1	2	3	4	5	6	7	8	9	OUT
REG.	401	377	190	386	336	531	158	355	386	3,120
PAR	4	4	3	4	4	5	3	4	4	35
HDCP	3	9	15	7	13	1	17	11	5	

HOLE	10	11	12	13	14	15	16	17	18	IN	TOTAL
REG.	386	145	384	404	308	317	108	510	390	2,952	6,072
PAR	4	3	4	4	4	4	3	5	4	35	70
HDCP	8	16	10	4	14	12	18	2	6		

RATES: Weekdays: nonresidents, $22; residents, $17; $13 after 3 p.m. Weekends: nonresidents, $25; residents, $20; $14 after 3 p.m. Carts: $22 for nonresidents, $18 for residents.
FACILITIES: Putting green, driving range, golf lessons, pro shop, restaurant, snack shop, bar, banquet facilities, locker rooms, golf equipment sold, tee time required.

WING PARK GOLF COURSE
WING STREET AND WING PARK BOULEVARD
ELGIN, IL 60120
(708)931-5952

9-Hole Course, 3,195 Yards, Par 36, CDGA rating N/A

LOCATION: ½ mile west of Route 31 on Wing Street

SEASON: April through October

GOLF PROFESSIONAL: Rick Bell

COURSE OWNER: City of Elgin

GREENS SUPERINTENDENT: Jack Hughes

Built in 1908, Wing Park is the oldest 9-hole municipal course in Illinois. Measured at just 3,195 yards, the course is very short. Fairways are wide open, and the greens are guarded by a few small bunkers. There are no water hazards, and the terrain largely consists of gently rolling hills. The course record of 29 is shared by several golfers.

SCORECARD:

HOLE	1	2	3	4	5	6	7	8	9	TOTAL
YARDS	310	389	300	355	190	577	470	447	157	3,195
PAR	4	4	4	4	3	5	5	4	3	36
HDCP	6	4	7	5	8	1	2	3	9	

RATES: Weekdays: $12 for 18, $7.50 for 9 and for twilight. Junior and senior rates available. Weekends: $17 for 18, $10 for 9 and for twilight. Carts: $20 for 18, $10 for 9.

FACILITIES: Golf lessons, pro shop, snack shop, club rental, golf equipment sold, tee time recommended. Shirts are required.

North

BONNIE BROOK GOLF COURSE
2800 NORTH LEWIS AVENUE
WAUKEGAN, IL 60087
(708)336-5538

18-Hole Course, 6,406 Yards, Par 72, CDGA rating 71.5
LOCATION: 35 miles north of the Loop along the lake
SEASON: Open all year
GOLF PROFESSIONAL: Marvin Rezabek
COURSE OWNER: Waukegan Park District
GREENS SUPERINTENDENT: Dave Beno

This course started out in 1926 as a private country club and was purchased in 1931 by the Waukegan Park District. Many new trees and bunkers have been added during the last 8 years, and 7 tees have been changed in the past 6 years. The course is heavily wooded, and water comes into play on 9 holes. The watered fairways are not too tight, and there are only a few fairway traps, but the trees, water, and thick rough provide plenty of hazards. The large greens are well trapped and have a lot of slope, making putting very tricky. This course can challenge the best player, but the average golfer will enjoy playing here as well.

SCORECARD:

HOLE	1	2	3	4	5	6	7	8	9	OUT
CHAMP.	513	333	183	407	515	184	362	374	382	3,253
REG.	501	326	159	400	503	167	349	361	362	3,128
WOMEN	480	299	135	382	482	144	334	350	341	2,947
PAR	5	4	3	4	5	3	4	4	4	36
HDCP	4	18	8	2	6	10	12	16	14	

HOLE	10	11	12	13	14	15	16	17	18	IN	TOTAL
CHAMP.	462	306	369	328	548	431	359	178	421	3,402	6,655
REG.	449	289	354	316	535	425	340	161	409	3,278	6,406
WOMEN	422	222	315	304	459	330	309	143	393	2,897	5,844
PAR	4	4	4	4	5	4	4	3	4	36	72
HDCP	1	17	9	15	5	3	11	13	7		

RATES: Weekdays: $16 for 18, $10 for 9 and after 3 p.m. Senior citizens (Monday and Tuesday): $13 for 18, $8 for 9. Weekends: $20 for 18, $14 for 9 and after 3 p.m. Resident rates available. Carts: weekdays, $16 for 18, $10 for 9; weekends, $19 for 18, $11 for 9.

FACILITIES: Putting green, driving range, golf lessons, pro shop, restaurant, snack shop, bar, banquet facilities, locker rooms, golf equipment sold, tee time recommended, permanent tee times available on weekends.

151

BRAE LOCH GOLF COURSE
33600 ROUTE 45
GRAYSLAKE, IL 60030
(708)223-5542

18-Hole Course, 5,872 Yards, Par 70, CDGA rating 66.8
LOCATION: 40 miles northwest of the Loop
SEASON: April through November
GOLF MANAGER: Dan Prezell
COURSE OWNER: Lake County Forest Preserve
GREENS SUPERINTENDENT: Tom Morgensen

This Lake County Forest Preserve District course has wide, flat fairways and appeals to the average golfer. Trees provide most of the trouble you'll encounter on this short, 18-hole layout. There are 4 water hazards—3 play laterally and 1 plays over—and 25 sand traps dot the fairways, surrounding several of the greens.

SCORECARD:

HOLE	1	2	3	4	5	6	7	8	9	OUT
WHITE	397	301	121	487	406	186	393	173	358	2,822
RED	387	271	111	411	382	176	383	163	350	2,634
PAR	4	4	3	5	4	3	4	3	4	34
HDCP	5	11	17	3	1	13	7	15	9	

HOLE	10	11	12	13	14	15	16	17	18	IN	TOTAL
WHITE	407	203	297	370	158	559	513	292	251	3,050	5,872
RED	395	193	287	362	148	549	505	274	239	2,952	5,586
PAR	4	3	4	4	3	5	5	4	4	36	70
HDCP	6	14	12	8	16	2	4	10	18		

RATES: Weekdays: $20 for 18, $16 for 9 and after 4 p.m. Weekends: $23 for 18, $20 for 9 and twilight. Resident rates available. Carts: $18 for 18, $12 for 9.
FACILITIES: Putting green, golf lessons, pro shop, restaurant, snack shop, bar, banquet facilities, club rental, permanent tee time available.

COUNTRYSIDE GOLF COURSE
ROUTE 60/83 AND HAWLEY ROAD
MUNDELEIN, IL 60060
(708)566-5544

18-Hole Course, 6,233 Yards, Par 73, CDGA rating 69.2
LOCATION: 35 miles northwest of the Loop
SEASON: April through November
GOLF MANAGER: Dan Prezell
COURSE OWNER: Lake County Forest Preserve
GREENS SUPERINTENDENT: Tom Morgensen

In 1976, the Lake County Forest Preserve District purchased this 18-hole golf course from the previous owner. Just over 6,000 yards from the white tees, the course is not too long, and the watered fairways are wide open. With a slope rating of 118, this layout, featuring some trees and 2 water holes, is ideal for the middle to high handicapper. The land is gently rolling, and there are several well-placed traps to attract your tee and approach shots to the green.

SCORECARD:

HOLE	1	2	3	4	5	6	7	8	9	OUT
WHITE	469	323	489	177	380	498	153	341	401	3,231
RED	414	309	479	171	368	386	141	277	391	2,936
PAR	5	4	5	3	4	5	3	4	4	37
HDCP	3	13	7	15	9	1	17	11	5	

HOLE	10	11	12	13	14	15	16	17	18	IN	TOTAL
WHITE	388	360	456	192	457	123	343	307	376	3,002	6,233
RED	377	341	428	185	427	116	333	272	367	2,846	5,782
PAR	4	4	5	3	5	3	4	4	4	36	73
HDCP	2	16	4	6	8	18	14	12	10		

RATES: Weekdays: residents: $12 for 18, $9 for 9; nonresidents: $20 for 18, $16 after 4 p.m. and for 9; senior citizen (62 or older) residents: $9 for 18, $7 for 9. Weekends: residents: $14 for 18, $11 for 9; nonresidents, $23 for 18, $20 for 9. Carts: $18 for 18, $12 for 9.

FACILITIES: Putting green, driving range, golf lessons, pro shop, snack shop, bar, club rental, permanent tee time available.

DEERPATH PARK GOLF COURSE
500 WEST DEERPATH ROAD
LAKE FOREST, IL 60045
(708)615-4290

18-Hole Course, 6,097 Yards, Par 70, CDGA rating 68.1
LOCATION: 30 miles north of Chicago
SEASON: April through November
GOLF PROFESSIONAL: Chris Marszalek
COURSE OWNER: City of Lake Forest
GREENS SUPERINTENDENT: Craig Joscelyn

Deerpath Park was built in 1927 and has always been a public course. Fairways are narrow, completely watered, and well trapped with a stream winding through the course, causing hazards on 4 holes. The terrain is basically flat, and there are not many trees. The greens are small, surrounded by sand traps on this well-maintained layout. The club's golf pro, Chris Marszalek, established the course record with a 61.

SCORECARD:

HOLE	1	2	3	4	5	6	7	8	9	OUT
MEN	366	362	492	335	175	425	297	184	369	3,005
WOMEN	355	353	425	231	145	381	282	167	351	2,690
PAR	4	4	5	4	3	4	4	3	4	35
HDCP	5	9	3	11	15	1	13	17	7	

HOLE	10	11	12	13	14	15	16	17	18	IN	TOTAL
MEN	371	339	533	193	377	161	413	336	369	3,092	6,097
WOMEN	356	257	518	168	364	146	396	316	350	2,871	5,561
PAR	4	4	5	3	4	3	4	4	4	35	70
HDCP	10	12	4	16	2	18	6	14	8		

RATES: Weekdays: $18 for 18, $13 for 9. Senior residents, $13 for 18. Weekends: $23 for 18, $15 for 9 and after 3 p.m. Resident rates available. Carts: $20 for 18, $12 for 9; seniors, $10 for 9, $16 for 18.
FACILITIES: Putting green, driving range, golf lessons, pro shop, restaurant, snack shop, bar, locker rooms, club rental, golf equipment sold.

FOSS PARK GOLF CLUB
3124 ARGONNE
NORTH CHICAGO, IL 60064
(708)689-1633

18-Hole Course, 6,839 Yards, Par 72, CDGA rating 70.8
LOCATION: Just off Route 41, north of Buckley Road
SEASON: April through November
GOLF PROFESSIONAL: Thomas K. Scott
GREENS SUPERINTENDENT: Bob Winter

Foss Park is a 6,839-yard course built in 1972 on rolling terrain. The grounds feature a few well-placed bunkers, and a creek runs through the course and comes into play on several holes. Foss Park is a good test of ability and will require you to use every club in your bag.

SCORECARD:

HOLE	1	2	3	4	5	6	7	8	9	OUT
BLUE	432	160	366	512	444	172	412	536	403	3,437
WHITE	411	148	344	490	422	155	390	516	381	3,257
RED	383	132	314	460	392	105	360	490	351	2,987
PAR	4	3	4	5	4	3	4	5	4	36
HDCP	5	17	13	9	1	15	3	7	11	

HOLE	10	11	12	13	14	15	16	17	18	IN	TOTAL
BLUE	411	513	212	414	400	177	486	368	421	3,402	6,839
WHITE	393	471	198	389	380	164	466	342	393	3,196	6,453
RED	369	453	180	355	354	146	401	244	322	2,824	5,811
PAR	4	5	3	4	4	3	5	4	4	36	72
HDCP	10	6	14	2	8	18	16	12	4		

RATES: Weekdays: nonresident, $15; resident, $10; seniors, $9; twilight, $9. Weekends: nonresident, $19; resident, $13; twilight, $12. Carts: weekdays, $15; weekends, $19.
FACILITIES: Putting green, driving range, golf lessons, pro shop, snack shop, bar, locker rooms, club rental, golf equipment sold, cart required, tee time recommended. Shirts and shoes must be worn in the clubhouse.

GLENVIEW PARK GOLF CLUB
800 SHERMER ROAD
GLENVIEW, IL 60025
(708)724-0250

18-Hole Course, 6,050 Yards, Par 70, CDGA rating 68.5
LOCATION: 25 miles northwest of the Loop
SEASON: March through December
GOLF PROFESSIONALS: David Rowlands and David Prange
COURSE OWNER: Glenview Park District
GREENS SUPERINTENDENT: Richard Wilson

This 18-hole golf course is a facility of the Glenview Park District, situated in a residential neighborhood. Although the course is classified as wide open, an abundance of trees line the watered fairways, and about 70 sand traps dot the fairways, surrounding the greens. Three water hazards also add to the challenge on this semihilly course which is always in excellent condition.

SCORECARD:

HOLE	1	2	3	4	5	6	7	8	9	OUT
REG.	323	398	404	416	414	183	553	307	180	3,178
WOMEN	301	375	384	400	399	172	531	290	164	3,016
PAR	4	4	4	4	4	3	5	4	3	35
HDCP	11	5	3	7	1	13	9	17	15	

HOLE	10	11	12	13	14	15	16	17	18	IN	TOTAL
REG.	193	374	381	339	320	348	477	122	318	2,872	6,050
WOMEN	176	362	360	331	306	335	453	110	302	2,735	5,751
PAR	3	4	4	4	4	4	5	3	4	35	70
HDCP	12	2	4	6	14	8	16	18	10		

RATES: Weekdays: $22 for 18, $13 for 9 and after 4 p.m. Weekends: $24 for 18, $14 after 3 p.m. Resident rates available. Carts: $20 for 18, $12 for 9.

FACILITIES: Putting green, golf lessons, pro shop, restaurant, bar, banquet facilities, locker rooms, club rental, golf equipment sold, tee time recommended.

HEATHER RIDGE GOLF CLUB
5900 HEATHER RIDGE DRIVE
GURNEE, IL 60031
(708)367-6010

9-Hole Course, 2,861 Yards, Par 35, CDGA rating N/A
LOCATION: Routes 120 and 21 in Lake County
SEASON: April through October
GOLF PROFESSIONAL: Tom McDonald
GREENS SUPERINTENDENT: Chris Smith

In 1974, the Heather Ridge Development Company designed and built this 9-hole, basically flat golf course. The fairways are very narrow, bordered on the left by houses and on the right by water all the way around the course. The tees, fairways, and greens are all watered with an automatic irrigation system, and the condition of the course is excellent. There are not many trees or traps to bother your shots, but the tight fairways reward the straight shooter.

SCORECARD:

HOLE	1	2	3	4	5	6	7	8	9	TOTAL
MEN	245	420	341	104	479	373	186	402	311	2,861
WOMEN	231	404	326	90	377	359	172	389	297	2,645
PAR	4	4	4	3	5	4	3	4	4	35
HDCP	8	1	3	9	5	6	4	2	7	

RATES: Weekdays: $9 for 9, $13.50 for 18. Weekends: $10.50 for 9, $15.50 for 18. Carts: weekdays, $11 for 9, $16 for 18; weekends, $12 for 9, $17 for 18. Resident rates available.
FACILITIES: Putting green, golf lessons, pro shop, snack shop, banquet facilities, club rental, golf equipment sold, tee time recommended.

HICKORY KNOLL GOLF COURSE
24745 WEST MONAVILLE ROAD
LAKE VILLA, IL 60046
(708)356-8640

9-Hole Course, 1,780 Yards, Par 30, CDGA rating N/A

LOCATION: 10 miles west of I-94, 1 mile south of Route 132

SEASON: April through November

GOLF PROFESSIONAL: Blair Subry

COURSE OWNERS: Joe Scarpelli, Bill Novice

GREENS SUPERINTENDENT: Ernie Scarpelli

Hickory Knoll is a good beginner's course. The fairways are wide open, and the longest hole is the 285-yard, par-4 6th. The terrain is mostly flat as are the small bent-grass greens. The course was built in 1949 and purchased by the current owners in 1975. Bill Cross set the course record of 29 in 1983.

SCORECARD:

HOLE	1	2	3	4	5	6	7	8	9	TOTAL
YARDS	240	180	265	210	160	285	135	140	165	1,780
PAR	4	3	4	3	3	4	3	3	3	30
HDCP	3	6	2	4	7	1	8	9	5	

RATES: Weekdays: $5; senior citizens, $4.25. Tuesdays: Ladies' Day, $4.25. Weekends: $6. Carts: $7; senior citizens on weekdays, $6; pullcarts, $1.

FACILITIES: Putting green, golf lessons, pro shop, club rental, golf equipment sold.

LAKE BLUFF GOLF CLUB
Illinois Highway 176 and Green Bay Road
Lake Bluff, IL 60044
(708)234-6771

18-Hole Course, 6,595 Yards, Par 72, CDGA rating 70.9
LOCATION: Green Bay Road and Route 176
SEASON: April through December
GOLF PROFESSIONAL: Chuck McDermand
COURSE OWNER: Lake Bluff Park District
GREENS SUPERINTENDENT: Jerry Mach

Lake Bluff is a park district course built in 1967. With 3 sets of tees to play from on each hole, this course offers a true test for golfers at any skill level. Water comes into play on 14 out of the 18 holes, and if you aren't hitting your ball into the water, there are plenty of sand traps and trees to worry about. The terrain is mostly flat, and fairways vary from narrow to wide open. In 1977, Dr. Gus James established the course record with a 64.

SCORECARD:

HOLE	1	2	3	4	5	6	7	8	9	OUT
BLUE	397	370	397	197	328	498	153	535	444	3,319
WHITE	389	370	390	185	328	498	141	535	393	3,229
RED	373	362	376	125	319	429	126	475	377	2,962
PAR	4	4	4	3	4	5	3	5	4	36
HDCP	9	15	7	11	13	3	17	1	5	

HOLE	10	11	12	13	14	15	16	17	18	IN	TOTAL
BLUE	430	479	393	162	510	204	319	365	414	3,276	6,595
WHITE	422	479	393	153	510	195	308	354	414	3,228	6,457
RED	413	470	323	138	502	171	292	336	398	3,043	6,005
PAR	4	5	4	3	5	3	4	4	4	36	72
HDCP	6	4	10	18	2	14	16	12	8		

RATES: Monday through Thursday: $19, $15 after 4 p.m. Friday through Sunday: $26, $18 after 4 p.m. Carts: $20. Resident rates available.
FACILITIES: Putting green, golf lessons, pro shop, restaurant, snack shop, banquet facilities, locker rooms, club rental, golf equipment sold, tee time recommended, permanent tee time available.

MARRIOTT'S LINCOLNSHIRE RESORT
10 MARRIOTT DRIVE
LINCOLNSHIRE, IL 60069
(708)634-5935

18-Hole Course, 6,296 Yards, Par 70, CDGA rating 71.2
LOCATION: 35 miles north of the Loop
SEASON: April 1 through November 15
DIRECTOR OF GOLF: Jim Zeh
COURSE OWNER: Marriott Hotels and Resorts
GREENS SUPERINTENDENT: Rick Hahn

This 18-hole course, owned and operated by Marriott Hotels and Resorts, was designed by George Fazio, who also designed Butler National Golf Club in Oak Brook. Since its inception in 1974, several greens on the back 9 have been redesigned by Ken Killian and Dick Nugent. The course is not too long—6,292 yards from the championship tees—but there are a lot of hazards. The Des Plaines River, Indian Creek, and 5 ponds beckon your ball to take a bath on 16 out of the 18 holes. The watered fairways are narrow, lined by water and trees, and there are plenty of fairway traps to catch your tee shots. The large, rolling greens are fast and tough to one-putt. Well-placed sand traps around the greens also make it difficult to pitch and roll; most of your approach shots will have to hit and hold the green to stay out of trouble. The resort is open all year, and the hotel accommodations, meeting rooms, and banquet facilities are second to none.

SCORECARD:

HOLE	1	2	3	4	5	6	7	8	9	OUT
BLUE	327	350	383	331	333	158	506	401	154	2,943
WHITE	310	339	370	326	322	117	477	387	133	2,781
YELLOW	280	270	316	311	300	100	371	286	89	2,323
PAR	4	4	4	4	4	3	5	4	3	35
HDCP	12	4	9	10	11	18	3	1	17	

HOLE	10	11	12	13	14	15	16	17	18	IN	TOTAL
BLUE	452	420	183	448	381	302	215	505	447	3,353	6,296
WHITE	444	371	175	432	366	293	205	486	441	3,213	5,994
YELLOW	374	345	112	353	349	276	140	473	338	2,760	5,083
PAR	4	4	3	4	4	4	3	5	4	35	70
HDCP	5	6	16	7	8	13	15	2	4		

RATES: April 1 through April 19: $35 for 18, $18 for 9. April 20 through October 6: Weekdays: $44 for 18, $25 for 9. Weekends: $48 for 18, $28 for 9. October 7 through November 15, $35 for 18, $18 for 9. Rates include carts, which are mandatory.

FACILITIES: Putting green, golf lessons, pro shop, restaurant, snack shop, bar, banquet facilities, locker rooms, club rental, golf equipment sold, cart required, tee time required.

MIDLANE COUNTRY CLUB
14565 YORK HOUSE ROAD
WADSWORTH, IL 60083
(708)244-1990

18-Hole Course, 6,736 Yards, Par 72, CDGA rating 72.8
LOCATION: 40 miles north of the Loop
SEASON: March through December
GOLF PROFESSIONAL: Howard Robinson
COURSE OWNER: Tom Rosenquist
GREENS SUPERINTENDENT: Brad Anderson

This is a very long and challenging golf course. Designed by Robert Harris, whose work includes such courses as Hillcrest in Illinois, Signal Point in Michigan, and the Country Club of Florida, Midlane was built in 1963 and opened as a private country club. This complete golfing facility offers several putting greens, a driving range, and banquet facilities for up to 350 people. Built on rolling hills, the fairways are narrow and completely watered. More than 200 trees and 6 lakes have been added in the past 4 years, and there are traps and bunkers on every hole making accuracy a must on this course. This is a beautiful public facility with a country-club atmosphere.

SCORECARD:

HOLE	1	2	3	4	5	6	7	8	9	OUT
GOLD	434	554	410	171	386	555	408	225	462	3,605
BLUE	415	533	388	161	370	540	389	202	447	3,445
WHITE	402	511	368	150	349	525	365	183	428	3,281
RED	362	461	343	139	309	452	295	153	415	2,929
PAR	4	5	4	3	4	5	4	3	4	36
HDCP	7	5	15	17	13	1	9	11	3	

HOLE	10	11	12	13	14	15	16	17	18	IN	TOTAL
GOLD	445	414	200	356	530	385	433	188	517	3,468	7,073
BLUE	420	391	184	332	510	368	408	172	506	3,291	6,736
WHITE	400	376	162	307	491	351	383	157	475	3,102	6,383
RED	372	353	120	236	419	316	322	133	435	2,706	5,635
PAR	4	4	3	4	5	4	4	3	5	36	72
HDCP	10	2	12	18	4	14	8	16	6		

RATES: Weekdays: before 9 a.m., $30; 9 a.m.–3 p.m., $38 (rates include carts which are required before 3 p.m.); $13 after 3 p.m. walking. Weekends: $45 includes cart, $15 after 3 p.m. walking.
FACILITIES: Putting green, driving range, golf lessons, pro shop, restaurant, snack shop, bar, banquet facilities, locker rooms, club rental, golf equipment sold, tee time required, permanent tee time available.

ORCHARD HILLS COUNTRY CLUB
38342 NORTH GREEN BAY ROAD
WAUKEGAN, IL 60087
(708)336-5118

18-Hole Course, 6,529 Yards, Par 72, CDGA rating 70.9
LOCATION: 40 miles north of Chicago
SEASON: Open all year except for the month of February.
GENERAL MANAGER: Pat Dinan
COURSE OWNERS: Leon Levithal and Walter Nathan
GREENS SUPERINTENDENT: Pat Dinan

Designed for the average golfer, Orchard Hills has wide-open fairways and flat terrain. Trees provide most of the hazards, and there are very few sand traps. Numbers 2, 3, 16, and 18 are the only water holes—3 play over the water and 1 plays laterally. Watered fairways were added in 1990, and the small to medium-sized greens have been enlarged annually for the past several years. The atmosphere is friendly and comfortable at this established course that has been a favorite of golfers in the Chicago area since its inception in 1922.

SCORECARD:

HOLE	1	2	3	4	5	6	7	8	9	OUT
MEN	423	491	363	412	151	512	177	367	422	3,318
WOMEN	403	458	353	402	141	492	167	357	405	3,178
PAR	4	5	4	4	3	5	3	4	4	36
HDCP	5	9	7	1	17	11	13	15	3	

HOLE	10	11	12	13	14	15	16	17	18	IN	TOTAL
MEN	397	412	377	144	509	357	349	198	468	3,211	6,529
WOMEN	377	402	367	135	464	347	304	193	418	3,007	6,185
PAR	4	4	4	3	5	4	4	3	5	36	72
HDCP	10	2	8	18	6	16	4	14	12		

RATES: Weekdays: $17 for 18, $10 after 3:30 p.m. Weekends: $20 for 18. Carts: weekdays, $17; weekends, $20.
FACILITIES: Putting green, practice range, golf lessons, pro shop, snack shop, bar, locker rooms, club rental, golf equipment sold, tee time required on weekends, permanent tee time available.

PETER N. JANS COMMUNITY GOLF COURSE
1031 CENTRAL STREET
EVANSTON, IL 60201
(708)475-9173

18-Hole Course, 3,608 Yards, Par 60, CDGA rating N/A
LOCATION: 3 miles east of Edens expressway
SEASON: Open year-round, weather permitting
GOLF PROFESSIONAL: Terry Govern
COURSE OWNER: Evanston/Wilmette Golf Course Association
GREENS SUPERINTENDENT: Terry Govern

The overall length at Peter Jans is suited to the high handicapper. The course runs north and south along the North Channel Sanitary Canal and is very scenic in some areas. The Baha'i Temple is visible just east of the 4th tee. Peter Jans opened as a public course in 1918, and over the years numerous tees have been rebuilt. The course record is a 4 under par 56 set by Frank Govern in 1955. Although the course is only 3,600 yards long, it is difficult to shoot par due to several long par 3s.

SCORECARD:

HOLE	1	2	3	4	5	6	7	8	9	OUT
YARDS	324	210	241	220	150	123	130	170	172	1,740
PAR	4	3	4	3	3	3	3	3	3	29
HDCP	7	3	13	2	11	16	15	5	6	

HOLE	10	11	12	13	14	15	16	17	18	IN	TOTAL
YARDS	260	115	157	236	140	305	270	189	196	1,868	3,608
PAR	4	3	3	4	3	4	4	3	3	31	60
HDCP	9	18	10	14	17	8	12	1	4		

RATES: Weekdays: $8, $6 after 4 p.m., $4 after 6 p.m.; senior citizens, $6; juniors after 1 p.m., $5. Weekends: $9, $6 after 4 p.m., $4 after 6 p.m. Carts: pull carts only, $2.
FACILITIES: Putting green, golf lessons, pro shop, snack shop, bar, banquet facilities, club rental, golf equipment sold, fivesomes allowed, tee time recommended, permanent tee time available.

PINE MEADOW GOLF CLUB
BUTTERFIELD ROAD AND LAKE STREET
MUNDELEIN, IL 60060
(708)566-4653

18-Hole Course, 6,614 Yards, Par 72, CDGA rating 71.7
LOCATION: One mile north of Illinois Highway 176
SEASON: April 1 through November
GOLF PROFESSIONAL: Joe Jemsek
COURSE OWNER: Joe Jemsek
GREENS SUPERINTENDENT: Tom Savage

Voted America's best new public course in 1986 by *Golf Digest*, Pine Meadow is a long and challenging championship-caliber course. It opened in August 1985 and was the site of the Illinois State Amateur Championship in 1987. The terrain is gently rolling, and 3 lakes come into play on 7 holes. The wide fairways have generous rough on either side, and the course is heavily wooded. Greens are large and well bunkered, and the 75 sand traps which dot the fairways and surround the greens offer plenty of challenges to even the most accurate shooter. The course also has a first-class driving range and target greens with sand traps. This beautiful 18-hole layout is truly a golfer's paradise.

SCORECARD:

HOLE	1	2	3	4	5	6	7	8	9	OUT
BLACK	378	556	472	537	245	432	454	196	380	3,650
BLUE	360	533	442	515	210	410	431	165	362	3,428
WHITE	343	511	418	476	164	382	416	131	342	3,183
RED	285	399	401	466	136	369	343	106	330	2,835
PAR	4	5	4	5	3	4	4	3	4	36
HDCP	11	1	5	3	15	7	9	17	13	

HOLE	10	11	12	13	14	15	16	17	18	IN	TOTAL
BLACK	394	370	195	541	393	563	405	178	440	3,479	7,129
BLUE	373	355	160	531	358	460	384	160	405	3,186	6,614
WHITE	355	347	128	492	328	448	353	150	377	2,978	6,161
RED	326	263	110	407	258	429	289	129	366	2,577	5,412
PAR	4	4	3	5	4	5	4	3	4	36	72
HDCP	12	14	16	2	8	4	10	18	6		

RATES: $44 for 18, $22 after 5 p.m. Carts: $23, $15 after 5 p.m.
FACILITIES: Putting green, driving range, golf lessons, pro shop, snack shop, bar, club rental, golf equipment sold, tee time recommended, permanent tee time available on Saturdays and Sundays.

RENWOOD COUNTRY CLUB
1413 HAINESVILLE ROAD
ROUND LAKE, IL 60073
(708)546-8242

18-Hole Course, 5,959 Yards, Par 72, CDGA rating 68.6
LOCATION: 5 miles west of I-294 at Route 120
SEASON: Mid-March through November
GOLF PROFESSIONAL: Diane Miller
COURSE OWNER: Round Lake Area Park District
GREENS SUPERINTENDENT: Sandy Bemis

Built in the early 1920s, Renwood started out as a private 9-hole club. It was purchased by one of the members in 1970 and then sold to the current owners in 1982. In 1974, the course grew from 9 holes to its current 18. The narrow fairways are bordered by trees or water, and many well-placed ponds make shot placement important. The greens are bent grass and vary in size from small on the front 9 to large on the back 9. The holes are not well bunkered, so there is room to get up and down if you miss the green. The average player should score well on this short layout.

SCORECARD:

HOLE	1	2	3	4	5	6	7	8	9	OUT
WHITE	345	388	376	152	344	496	390	307	481	3,279
RED	327	376	346	126	312	450	356	281	401	2,975
PAR	4	4	4	3	4	5	4	4	5	37
HDCP	7	3	5	15	13	11	1	17	9	

HOLE	10	11	12	13	14	15	16	17	18	IN	TOTAL
WHITE	135	352	293	270	295	168	503	334	330	2,680	5,959
RED	117	323	278	256	283	148	489	327	318	2,539	5,514
PAR	3	4	4	4	4	3	5	4	4	35	72
HDCP	18	2	14	16	12	6	4	10	8		

RATES: Weekdays: $15, $9 after 3 p.m., $6 after 6 p.m. Weekends: $19, $14 after 3 p.m., $6 after 6 p.m. Carts: $19 for 18, $11 for 9.
FACILITIES: Putting green, driving range, golf lessons, pro shop, restaurant, snack shop, bar, banquet facilities, locker rooms, club rental, golf equipment sold, tee time recommended. The dress code requires that shirts and shoes be worn at all times.

SPORTSMAN COUNTRY CLUB
3535 DUNDEE ROAD
NORTHBROOK, IL 60062
(708)291-2350

18-Hole Course, 6,354 Yards, Par 70, CDGA rating 69.7
9-Hole East Course, 3,016 Yards, Par 35, CDGA rating 34.4
LOCATION: 20 miles north of the Loop
SEASON: Open all year
GOLF PROFESSIONAL: Mark Robertson
COURSE OWNER: Northbrook Park District
GREENS SUPERINTENDENT: Kevin Czerkies

This scenic 18-hole course is not too long, but the combination of majestic tree-lined fairways, 6 water hazards, and 75 sand traps offers severe challenges to your scoring ability. The terrain varies from flat to gently rolling, and the greens are elevated and well bunkered. The fairways were recently changed to bent grass, and several tees were rebuilt. The 9-hole east course designed by Roger Packard opened in June of 1991. Several ponds and lakes come into play on this 3,016-yard, classically styled course. The greens are protected either by well-placed bunkers or water, and the bent-grass fairways are wide enough to give your driver a test. Sportsman Country Club opened in 1922 and has had several proprietors over the years, but it is currently owned and operated by the Northbrook Park District.

18-HOLE SCORECARD:

HOLE	1	2	3	4	5	6	7	8	9	OUT
BLUE	483	402	174	386	381	153	488	212	461	3,140
WHITE	455	380	161	382	368	138	477	204	458	3,023
RED	418	360	143	376	355	118	462	138	454	2,824
PAR	5	4	3	4	4	3	5	3	4	35
HDCP	9	3	15	13	11	17	5	7	1	

HOLE	10	11	12	13	14	15	16	17	18	IN	TOTAL
BLUE	164	403	428	373	176	413	297	531	429	3,214	6,354
WHITE	136	395	418	359	166	401	278	508	415	3,076	6,099
RED	98	385	405	340	153	384	253	490	396	2,904	5,728
PAR	3	4	4	4	3	4	4	5	4	35	70
HDCP	16	10	8	12	14	6	18	2	4		

EAST COURSE SCORECARD:

HOLE	1	2	3	4	5	6	7	8	9	OUT
BLUE	351	370	168	355	522	368	358	139	385	3,016
WHITE	337	341	149	327	500	340	346	125	367	2,832
RED	323	320	130	309	477	322	334	103	349	2,667
PAR	4	4	3	4	5	4	4	3	4	35
HDCP	13	7	15	11	3	5	9	17	1	

RATES: Weekdays: $23 for 18, $13 for East 9. Weekends: $25 for 18, $16 for East 9. Carts: $18 for 18, $9 for 9.

FACILITIES: Five putting greens, driving range, golf lessons, pro shop, snack shop, bar, banquet facilities, club rental, golf equipment sold, tee time recommended, permanent tee time available for residents only on weekends.

SUNSET VALLEY GOLF COURSE
1390 SUNSET ROAD
HIGHLAND PARK, IL 60035
(708)432-7140

18-Hole Course, 6,401 Yards, Par 72, CDGA rating 70.2
LOCATION: ½ mile west of the Edens expressway on Route 41
SEASON: April 1 through December 1
GOLF PROFESSIONAL: Tony Moseley
COURSE OWNER: Highland Park Park District
GREENS SUPERINTENDENT: Brian Green

Since its inception in 1922, Sunset Valley has been a public course owned by the Park District of Highland Park. This course is characterized by flat, long, narrow fairways, and many of the greens are small with traps in front, requiring them to be hit on the fly. There are 3 par 4s over 400 yards long, and a creek cuts through the course, requiring you to hit over water on 7 holes. The men's slope rating of 121 indicates the challenging nature of the course, although the average golfer will enjoy playing here. The course record is 64, established in 1985 by Bob Mark.

SCORECARD:

HOLE	1	2	3	4	5	6	7	8	9	OUT
MEN	337	500	359	140	412	153	516	357	367	3,141
WOMEN	316	420	344	130	342	144	507	342	348	2,893
PAR	4	5	4	3	4	3	5	4	4	36
HDCP	5	3	13	17	1	15	7	11	9	

HOLE	10	11	12	13	14	15	16	17	18	IN	TOTAL
MEN	351	164	516	374	205	400	413	493	344	3,260	6,401
WOMEN	339	141	493	355	164	393	401	483	333	3,102	5,995
PAR	4	3	5	4	3	4	4	5	4	36	72
HDCP	6	16	8	14	12	4	2	18	10		

RATES: Weekdays: $18 for 18, $14 after 2:30 p.m., $11 after 6 p.m. Senior citizens: $14 all day. Weekends: $24 for 18, $18 after 2:30 p.m., $13 after 6 p.m. Carts: $14 for 9, $22 for 18.
FACILITIES: Putting green, golf lessons, pro shop, snack shop, bar, locker rooms, club rental, golf equipment sold, tee time recommended, permanent tee time available.

VERNON HILLS GOLF COURSE
291 Evergreen Drive
Vernon Hills, IL 60010
(708)680-9310

9-Hole Course, 2,828 Yards, Par 34, CDGA rating 64.5
LOCATION: Route 45 and Evergreen Drive
SEASON: April through Thanksgiving weekend
GOLF PROFESSIONAL: Mark Psensky
COURSE OWNER: Village of Vernon Hills
GREENS SUPERINTENDENT: Mike McDonald

Vernon Hills measures only 2,828 yards from the back tees, but 3 of its 9 holes are 400-yard par 4s. A creek winds through the course creating hazards on 6 holes. A pond on number 7 requires a tee shot over water to a small, slightly contoured green. The course was built in 1980 and is well suited to the average player.

SCORECARD:

HOLE	1	2	3	4	5	6	7	8	9	TOTAL
BACK	368	319	165	279	410	332	137	407	411	2,828
FRONT	307	311	83	265	394	213	101	393	399	2,466
PAR	4	4	3	4	4	4	3	4	4	34
HDCP	7	13	11	15	3	9	17	1	5	

RATES: Weekdays: $13 for 18, $9 for 9, $3 off for juniors and seniors. Weekends: $15 for 18, $10 for 9, $3 off for juniors and seniors. Carts: $15 for 18, $10 for 9.
FACILITIES: Putting green, golf lessons, pro shop, snack shop, club rental, golf equipment sold, tee time recommended.

WEBER PARK GOLF COURSE
9300 NORTH BRONX
SKOKIE, IL 60077
(708)674-1510

9-Hole Course, 1,165 Yards, Par 27, CDGA rating N/A

LOCATION: 20 miles northwest of the Loop

SEASON: April 1 through December 1

GOLF PROFESSIONAL: Lee Dreuth

COURSE OWNER: Skokie Park District

GREENS SUPERINTENDENT: John Otis

This par-3, 9-hole golf course is ideal for the novice golfer. Located behind the Skokie Skatium Ice Skating Arena, Weber Park is described as "a nice little course" by the regulars who play here. The condition of the course has improved greatly over the past few years due to better maintenance, and trees have been planted yearly to make it more challenging. The watered fairways are narrow, and the lone "water" hazard is actually filled with stones rather than water to prevent excessive ball loss. The course is 17 years old, and the record of 22 was set by Lee Dreuth a few years ago.

SCORECARD:

HOLE	1	2	3	4	5	6	7	8	9	TOTAL
YARDS	135	130	140	100	105	195	130	110	120	1,165
PAR	3	3	3	3	3	3	3	3	3	27
HDCP	3	5	2	9	8	1	4	7	6	

RATES: Weekdays: $4.75; seniors, $4; 10–15 year olds, $4 until 3:30 p.m. Weekends: $5.25, replays $2.75.

FACILITIES: Putting green, golf lessons, snack shop, club rental.

Course Index

172

Glenview Park Golf Club, Glenview, 156
Glenwoodie Club, Glenwood, 30
Golf Club of Illinois, Algonquin, 123
Green Garden Country Club, Frankfort, 31
Heather Ridge Golf Club, Gurnee, 157
Hickory Creek Golf Course, Frankfort, 72
Hickory Hills Country Club, Hickory Hills, 32
Hickory Knoll Golf Course, Lake Villa, 158
Highland Woods Golf Course, Hoffman Estates, 17
Hilldale Country Club, Hoffman Estates, 124
Indian Boundary Golf Course, Chicago, 18
Indian Lakes Resort, Bloomingdale, 73
Inwood Golf Course, Joliet, 75
Jackson Park Golf Course, Chicago, 4
Joe Louis Golf Course, Riverdale, 19
Kemper Lakes, Hawthorn Woods, 125
Lake Bluff Golf Club, Lake Bluff, 159
Lake Park Golf Course, Des Plaines, 126
Lincoln Oaks Golf Course, Crete, 34
Longwood Country Club, Steger, 35
Marengo Ridge Golf and Country Club, Marengo, 127
Marquette Park Golf Course, Chicago, 5
Marriott's Lincolnshire Resort, Lincolnshire, 160
McArthur Municipal Golf Course, East Chicago, Indiana, 36
Meadow Lark Golf Course, Hinsdale, 20
Midlane Country Club, Wadsworth, 162
Minnie Monesse Golf Club, Grant Park, 37
Naperbrook Golf Course, Naperville, 76
Nordic Hills Resort, Itasca, 77
Oak Brook Hills, Oak Brook, 78
Oak Hills Country Club, Palos Heights, 79
Oak Meadows Golf Course, Addison, 80
Oak Springs Golf Club, St. Anne, 38
Old Oak Country Club, Orland Park, 81
Old Orchard Golf Course, Mt. Prospect, 129
Orchard Hills Country Club, Waukegan, 163
Palatine Hills Golf Course, Palatine, 130
Palmira Golf Course, St. John, Indiana, 39
Palos Country Club, Palos Park, 82
Par 3 Golf Club, LaGrange, 84
Peter N. Jans Golf Course, Evanston, 164
Pheasant Run Resort, St. Charles, 85
Phillips Park Golf Course, Aurora, 86

Pinecrest Golf and Country Club, Huntley, 131
Pine Meadow Golf Club, Mundelein, 165
Pistakee Country Club, McHenry, 132
Plum Tree National Golf Course, Harvard, 133
Poplar Creek Country Club, Hoffman Estates, 134
Pottawatomie Golf Course, St. Charles, 87
Prestbury Golf Club, Sugar Grove, 88
Ramada O'Hare Golf Course, Rosemont, 136
Randall Oaks Golf Club, Dundee, 137
Renwood Country Club, Round Lake, 166
River Oaks Golf Course, Calumet City, 21
Robert A. Black Golf Course, Chicago, 6
Rob Roy Golf Course, Prospect Heights, 138
Rolling Knolls Country Club, Elgin, 139
St. Andrews Golf and Country Club, West Chicago, 89
Salt Creek Golf Club, Wood Dale, 91
Schaumburg Golf Club, Schaumburg, 140
Scherwood Golf, Shererville, 40
Seven Bridges Golf Club, Woodridge, 92
Shady Lawn Golf Course, Beecher, 42
Shamrock Golf Course, St. Anne, 44
Silver Lakes Country Club, Orland Park, 45
South Gleason Golf Course, Gary, Indiana, 47
South Shore Country Club, Chicago, 7
South Shore Golf Club, Momence, 48
Spartan Meadows Golf Course, Elgin, 141
Sportsman Country Club, Northbrook, 167
Springbrook Golf Course, Naperville, 94
Sunset Valley Golf Course, Highland Park, 169
Sydney A. Marovitz Golf Course, Chicago, 8
Tamarack Golf Course, Naperville, 95
Thunderbird Country Club, Barrington, 142
Timber Trails Country Club, LaGrange, 97
Tuckaway Golf Course, Crete, 49
Twin Ponds Golf Course, Crystal Lake, 143
Urban Hills Country Club, Richton Park, 50
Valley Green Golf Course, North Aurora, 98
Vernon Hills Golf Course, Vernon Hills, 170
Village Greens of Woodridge, Woodridge, 99
Village Links of Glen Ellyn, Glen Ellyn, 100
Villa Olivia Country Club, Bartlett, 144
Walnut Greens, Schaumburg, 145
Weber Park Golf Course, Skokie, 171

Regional Index

175

Springbrook Golf Course, Naperville, 94
Tamarack Golf Course, Naperville, 95
Timber Trails Country Club, LaGrange, 97
Valley Green Golf Course, North Aurora, 98
Village Greens of Woodridge, Woodridge, 99
Village Links of Glen Ellyn, Glen Ellyn, 100
Wedgewood Golf Course, Joliet, 102
Westgate Valley Country Club, Palos Heights, 103
Willow Run Country Club, Mokena, 105
Woodbine Golf Course, Lockport, 106
Woodruff Golf Course, Joliet, 107
Zigfield Troy Golf Course, Woodridge, 108

NORTHWEST

Apple Orchard Golf Course, Bartlett, 111
Arboretum Golf Club, Buffalo Grove, 112
Arlington Lakes Golf Course, Arlington Heights, 113
Bonnie Dundee Golf and Country Club, Dundee, 114
Bristol Oaks Country Club, Bristol, Wisconsin, 115
Buffalo Grove Golf Course, Buffalo Grove, 116
Cary Country Club, Cary, 117
Chapel Hill Country Club, McHenry, 118
Chevy Chase Golf Course, Wheeling, 119
Crystal Woods Golf Course, Woodstock, 120
Fox Lake Country Club, Fox Lake, 121
Fox Run Golf Links, Elk Grove Village, 122
Golf Club of Illinois, Algonquin, 123
Hilldale Country Club, Hoffman Estates, 124
Kemper Lakes, Hawthorn Woods, 125
Lake Park Golf Course, Des Plaines, 126
Marengo Ridge Golf and Country Club, Marengo, 127
Old Orchard Golf Course, Mt. Prospect, 129
Palatine Hills Golf Course, Palatine, 130
Pinecrest Golf and Country Club, Huntley, 131
Pistakee Country Club, McHenry, 132
Plum Tree National Golf Course, Harvard, 133
Poplar Creek Country Club, Hoffman Estates, 134
Ramada O'Hare Golf Course, Rosemont, 136
Randall Oaks Golf Club, Dundee, 137
Rob Roy Golf Course, Prospect Heights, 138
Rolling Knolls Country Club, Elgin, 139
Schaumburg Golf Club, Schaumburg, 140
Spartan Meadows Golf Course, Elgin, 141
Thunderbird Country Club, Barrington, 142

Twin Ponds Golf Course, Crystal Lake, 143
Villa Olivia Country Club, Bartlett, 144
Walnut Greens, Schaumburg, 145
Wilmette Golf Course, Wilmette, 146
Wing Park Golf Course, Elgin, 147
NORTH
Bonnie Brook Golf Course, Waukegan, 151
Brae Loch Golf Course, Grayslake, 152
Countryside Golf Course, Mundelein, 153
Deerpath Park Golf Course, Lake Forest, 154
Foss Park Golf Club, North Chicago, 155
Glenview Park Golf Club, Glenview, 156
Heather Ridge Golf Club, Gurnee, 157
Hickory Knoll Golf Course, Lake Villa, 158
Lake Bluff Golf Club, Lake Bluff, 159
Marriott's Lincolnshire Resort, Lincolnshire, 160
Midlane Country Club, Wadsworth, 162
Orchard Hills Country Club, Waukegan, 163
Peter N. Jans Golf Course, Evanston, 164
Pine Meadow Golf Club, Mundelein, 165
Renwood Country Club, Round Lake, 166
Sportsman Country Club, Northbrook, 167
Sunset Valley Golf Course, Highland Park, 169
Vernon Hills Golf Course, Vernon Hills, 170
Weber Park Golf Course, Skokie, 171